Introducing

MODERN
MUSIC

Ottó Károlyi

PENGUIN BOOKS

PENGUIN BOOKS

Published by the Penguin Group
Penguin Books Ltd, 27 Wrights Lane, London w8 5tz, England
Penguin Books USA Inc., 375 Hudson Street, New York, New York 10014, USA
Penguin Books Australia Ltd, Ringwood, Victoria, Australia
Penguin Books Canada Ltd, 10 Alcorn Avenue, Toronto, Ontario, Canada m4v 3b2
Penguin Books (NZ) Ltd, 182–190 Wairau Road, Auckland 10, New Zealand

Penguin Books Ltd, Registered Offices: Harmondsworth, Middlesex, England

First published 1995

10 9 8 7 6 5 4 3 2 1

The moral right of the author has been asserted

The permissions on pp. xiii–xv constitute an extension of this copyright page

Set in 10.25/13 pt Monotype Bembo
Typeset by Datix International Limited, Bungay, Suffolk
Music setting by Barnes Music Engraving
Illustrations by Nigel Andrews
Printed in England by Clays Ltd, St Ives plc

To Benedikte and Julian

Contents

Preface

For most music lovers modern music is still a hard nut to crack. Bewilderment and dislike are often mixed with a sense of being provoked, if not conned. When the music is complex, it is referred to as élitist and incomprehensibly intellectual. When it is based on some simple idea, it is seen as superficial and primitive, and the all too common reaction is 'I could have done it'. One could, of course, postulate that the difference between an artist and a layman is that the former actually does what the latter thinks he or she could do, but does not. There is also the recurrent concern about 'noise', 'dissonance', 'tension' and so on, which put off so many listeners. To seek primarily diversion and solace in music, or in any art, is to misunderstand fundamentally its complex nature. It is for this reason that Santayana, in his book *Reason in Art*, wrote: 'A musical education is necessary for musical judgement. What most people relish is hardly music; it is, rather, a drowsy reverie relieved by nervous thrills.' Soothing is only one possible effect among many available to those whose craft it is to manipulate or, as Varèse put it, to 'organize sounds' in a meaningful way. The word 'manipulate' is used to emphasize the artificial in music whether modern or not. There is very little of the 'natural' in composing a symphony. On the contrary, it is an extremely artificial activity involving considerable technical know-how. Hence the truism that 'composing is ten per cent inspiration and ninety per cent perspiration'.

It has long been my belief that some technical understanding leads to a sympathetic and informed interest in what an artist is trying to do and express in his or her style. Moreover, dislike of a work of art is often based not so much on well-informed taste and opinion as on fear of the new, which results in the defensive blocking off of both mind and emotion. As far as the arts are concerned, it would be better to replace the saying 'I know what I like' with 'I don't know what I could like'.

This book, like *Introducing Music*, to which it is a sequel, offers the tools for a basic understanding, but of modern rather than traditional music. It hopes to provide the reader with some technical awareness of what happens when a twentieth-century composition is being performed. It should be remembered, however, that no amount of reading can substitute for the real thing: live music. It is a worthwhile investment to do a little homework before and after a concert; familiarity dispels anxiety. Technical terms in music can be absorbed in the same way as they are in computing, football, cricket, chess, card games and so forth. All artists are seekers of communication, and our task as the audience is to take part in the creative process by deciphering the signs, the means and methods of what is communicated to us. Remember what Gershwin said: 'Many people say that too much study kills spontaneity in Music, but although study may kill a small talent, it must develop a big one.'

Acknowledgements

I should like to thank all those who, with their good advice and constructive criticism, have significantly contributed to the realization of this book. I am particularly indebted to the professional help of Stefan McGrath, Ravi Mirchandani, Andrew Barker and Andrew Cameron of Penguin Books and to Helen Jeffrey.

I should also like to express my thanks to Elspeth Gillespie and Susan Sinclaire of the University of Stirling for their infinite patience in retyping the manuscript.

My warmest thanks, of course, go to my wife, Benedikte, and son, Julian, whose loving support is my daily bread – to them this book is dedicated.

Ottó Károlyi

Permissions

The author and publisher are grateful to the publishers who have given permission to reproduce copyright material:

Maurice Ravel: *Daphnis et Chloé,* copyright © 1934, *Ma mère l'oye,* copyright © 1925, String Quartet in F major, copyright © 1910: reproduced by permission of Arima Ltd & Editions Durand SA, Paris/United Music Publishers Ltd.

Earle Brown: *December;* Elliott Carter: String Quartet No. 2, copyright © 1951 (renewed) by Associated Music Publishers, Inc. (BMI); Henry Cowell: *The Hero Sun,* copyright © 1928 (renewed) by Associated Music Publishers, Inc. (BMI); Charles Ives: *Concord Sonata,* copyright © 1947 (renewed) by Arrow Music Press, Inc., Psalm 67, copyright © 1939 (renewed) by Arrow Music Press, Inc.; Maurice Ravel: *Pavane pour une infante défunte:* reproduced by permission of Associated Music Publishers, Inc. (BMI). International copyright secured. All rights reserved.

Béla Bartók: Concerto for Orchestra, *Divertimento, Mikrokosmos* (Vol. IV Nos 100, 102, 107, 109, 115; Vol. V Nos 127, 132; Vol. VI Nos 140, 146), Piano Concerto No. 3, *Ten Easy Pieces* ('Evening in the Country'); Benjamin Britten: Passacaglia from *Peter Grimes, The Young Person's Guide to the Orchestra;* Aaron Copland: *Billy the Kid, El salón México;* Peter Maxwell Davies: Symphony No. 3; Zoltán Kodály: Variations on a Hungarian

Folksong ('The Peacock'); Sergei Prokofiev, Classical Symphony Op. 25; Richard Strauss: *Elektra*, *Salome*; Igor Stravinsky: *Agon*, *In memoriam Dylan Thomas*, *Petrushka*, *The Rake's Progress*, *The Rite of Spring*, Symphonies of Wind Instruments, Symphony of Psalms: reproduced by permission of Boosey & Hawkes Music Publishers Ltd.

Krzysztof Penderecki: *Threnody to the Victims of Hiroshima*: reproduced by permission of CPP/Belwin Europe.

Claude Debussy: *Pelléas et Mélisande*, copyright © 1904; Olivier Messiaen: *Quatuor pour la fin du temps*, copyright © 1942: reproduced by permission of Editions Durand SA, Paris/United Music Publishers Ltd.

George Gershwin: 'Summertime': reproduced by permission of International Music Publishing.

Luigi Dallapiccola: 'Die Sonne kommt!': copyright © 1953 by Edizioni Suvini Zerboni, Milan.

William Walton: *Façade*, copyright © 1938 Oxford University Press: reproduced by kind permission of Oxford University Press.

John Cage: *A Room*, copyright © 1968 by Henmar Press Inc., New York; Morton Feldman: *Last Pieces*, copyright © 1963 by C. F. Peters Corporation, New York; Richard Strauss: *Also sprach Zarathustra*: reproduced by permission of Peters Edition Ltd, London.

Maurice Ravel: *Jeux d'eau*, copyright © 1944 (renewed) by G. Schirmer, Inc. (ASCAP); Arnold Schoenberg: String Quartet Op. 37 No. 4, copyright © 1939 (renewed) by G. Schirmer, Inc. (ASCAP); *A Survivor from Warsaw*: reproduced by permission of G. Schirmer, Inc. (ASCAP). International copyright secured. All rights reserved.

Peter Maxwell Davies: *O magnum mysterium*; Paul Hindemith: *Ludus tonalis*; Michael Tippett: Concerto for double string orchestra: reproduced by permission of Schott & Co. Ltd, London.

Béla Bartók: *Allegro barbaro*, Music for Strings, Percussion and

From Tonality to Atonality: *tonality, atonality, scales, melody, harmony, serialism, counterpoint (texture)*

> The formation of scales and the web of harmony is a product of artistic invention and is in no way given by the natural structure or by the natural behaviour of our hearing, as used to be generally maintained hitherto.
>
> HERMANN VON HELMHOLTZ

The loss of tonality, the loss of the familiar, is one of the most prominent factors which perturb most listeners. The change from tonal to atonal music is arguably the most striking feature of twentieth-century music. It is therefore appropriate that we turn first to the discussion of tonality and atonality.

Tonality

In tonal music all the notes of a scale gravitate towards the tonic or key note. In C major, for example, such notes as F (subdominant), G (dominant) and B (leading note) function hierarchically in relation to the pull of the fundamental note, the tonic or key note (see Fig. 1).

Tonic   Supertonic   Mediant   Subdominant   Dominant   Submediant   Leading note   Tonic

Fig. 1

Circle of fifths

Our scale system is based on the calculations of equal temperament (see p. 110). The circle of fifths is an indication of the practicality of that calculation in terms of tuning, modulation and keyboard instrument making. The principal idea of the circle of fifths is to arrive at a new key by moving either up a fifth (for example C G D A) or down a fifth (for example Eb Bb F C). In reality only seven upward moves of fifths and seven downward moves of fifths are of practical use; but in theory it is possible to continue and close the circle with the two notes which meet enharmonically (for

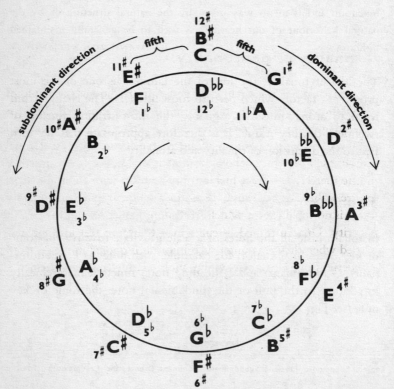

Fig. 2

instance B♯ and C, which are the same in sound, or the same note on the keyboard) after twelve sharps or flats (see Fig. 2).

Each key arrived at via the circle of fifths represents a tonal centre (C major or minor, G major or minor and so on). The tonic of each key has a gravitational pull to which the music returns home as it moves (see Fig. 3, from Beethoven's Symphony No. 5); hence the common reference to a home key. This is what gives tonal music its acousto-psychological stability.

Fig. 3

Atonality or pantonality

In atonal music, as its name suggests, the traditional principle of gravitational pull to the tonic or home key is discarded. What is offered instead is a chromatic freedom in which notes are organized in a way that avoids most of the characteristic features of tonal music, such as tonic, octave, dominant or leading notes. In tonal music there is a distinct hierarchy of sounds, with the tonic at its centre. With atonal music all notes are equal, and consequently there is no tonal centre. Much freedom is gained, but at the cost of security. Unaccustomed listeners may therefore feel lost and un-settled when they encounter such music as is quoted in Fig. 4, from Webern's Songs for voice, violin, viola, clarinet and bass clarinet.

von nun___ an bis in   E - wig - keit!

Fig. 4

Schoenberg, who was one of the foremost exponents of atonality, felt uneasy about the term 'atonality', since he thought it could be interpreted as devoid of tonality. He preferred to call the style pantonal; hence pantonality. In general parlance, though, it is atonality which seems to have established itself.

Scales

We have already seen that a series of pitches can be arranged to make up a scale – that is, notes built in progression from any note to its octave. In tonal music the scale of C major is C'D'E^{s}F'G'A'B^{s}C. This scale is made up of two whole tones + one semitone + three whole tones + one semitone, which is the pattern for all major diatonic scales. The word 'diatonic' (Greek *dia tonos* = proceeding by tones, that is, within an octave the intervallic combination of five whole tones and two semitones) refers to the fact that the C major scale can be played exclusively on the white keys of the piano, without chromatic notes. As long as the pattern of tones and semitones remains the same, the corresponding scales in each key will remain diatonic majors (see Fig. 5).

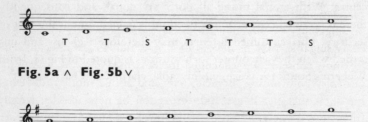

Fig. 5a ∧ **Fig. 5b** ∨

Minor scales are also structured by specific patterns, of which there are three types: natural minor (Fig. 6a), melodic minor (Fig. 6b) and harmonic minor (Fig. 6c).

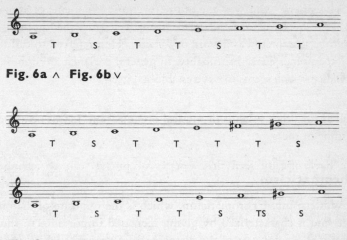

Fig. 6a ∧ **Fig. 6b** ∨

Fig. 6c

It should be remembered that the relationship between a scale and real music is like that between a skeleton and a living body.

Melody

Tonal melodies are primarily a horizontal manipulation of pitches based upon a scale pattern. Our musical tradition, which is largely founded on that of the eighteenth and nineteenth centuries, focuses on singability or tunefulness. The idea that a melody may not be easily singable, may be devoid of all tunefulness, is rather difficult for most conservatively inclined listeners to digest. An additional difficulty confronting listeners, over and above modern developments, is that the influx and absorption of new idioms, largely from non-Western countries, make further demands on their ears. Many melodies of this century belong to an unfamiliar type in terms of pitch, intervallic contour, rhythm and so forth, as the quotation from Schoenberg's Violin Concerto in Fig. 7 shows.

In order to enlarge their musical vocabulary composers searched for various developments within the traditional tonal system, as

Fig. 7

well as for other systems of musical organization. Let us now look at some of these.

Chromaticism

In Western music chromaticism, which is the opposite of diatonicism and is characterized by giving increased importance to those notes that are not part of the diatonic scales proper (such as, in the diatonic scale of C major, C♯ and D♯), goes back to as early as the ancient Greeks. A vogue for chromaticism developed, however, during the sixteenth century and opened up possibilities for musical expression of the most subtle kind for composers from the madrigalists to Wagner and beyond. When writing chromatic notes, the tendency is to sharpen notes going upwards and flatten

Fig. 8a ∧ **Fig. 8b** ∨

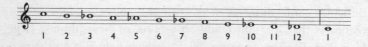

those going downwards (see Fig. 8). Fig. 9 gives some examples of chromatic thinking from Gesualdo to Debussy. By now our ears and minds have absorbed these and many more chromatic passages. The common trouble usually begins when we are confronted with

Fig. 9a Gesualdo: *Moro lasso*

Fig. 9b Bach: Fugue No. XII in F minor, *Das Wohltemperirte Clavier* Bk 1

Langsam und schmachtend

Fig. 9c Wagner: *Tristan und Isolde*

Très modéré (M.M. ♩ = 44)

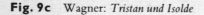

p doux et expressif

Fig. 9d Debussy: *Prélude à l'après-midi d'un faune*

Fig. 10

such atonal chromaticism as is found in the first of Webern's Six Songs (see Fig. 10).

No short cut can be offered to overcome the emotional difficulties. It is essential to hear the music several times in order to become familiar with it and to understand its basic principles. In the 1960s and 1970s 'difficult', new compositions were, from time to time, performed twice at the same concert. This practice, largely associated with Boulez, should be made a regular feature of our concert life.

Pentatonic scale

The pentatonic scale (five notes to an octave: C D E G A) is one of the most ancient and widespread scale structures in the world. Much folk music is based on it, in countries as far apart as Scotland and China. There are several types of pentatonic scale patterns in use (for example the Japanese equidistant pentatonic scale) in addition to the most popular one shown here. For modern composers its main fascination is that there is no real pull towards a tonic since the scale contains no semitones. The tonality is therefore rather ambivalent. By arranging the five notes of the basic scale starting, say, on c′, one gains five-note scale patterns (see Fig. 11).

Fig. 11

A fine illustration of the pentatonic scale in modern music is Bartók's 'Evening in the Country' for piano (see Fig. 12). Examples are plentiful in the music not only of those who were involved with nationalism (Mussorgsky, Dvořák) or folk music research (Bartók, Kodály), but also of Debussy and Ravel.

Fig. 12a

Fig. 12b

Modality

Some composers found another way of liberating themselves from the eighteenth- and nineteenth-century domination of tonal music by turning back to well before the time of tonal music, namely 1600. Music written during the Middle Ages and the Renaissance was based on a system of scale patterns called modes. The origin of the modal scale system and, indeed, the origin of our European scale systems can be traced to the ancient Greeks. It was they who gave tribal names to their scales, such as Dorian, Phrygian and Lydian. Each of these also had a subordinate scale companion, starting a fifth below it, which was distinguished by the prefix 'hypo', meaning 'under' (see Fig. 13). Thus the subordinate scale of Dorian, for example, was called Hypodorian. The Greeks worked out their scales in descending order.

Fig. 13

During the Middle Ages Christian musicians and theoreticians took over the Greek scales, but because of an obscure misunderstanding they began their modes on D, E, F and G. Unlike the Greeks, they took their scales in ascending order, and consequently the Phrygian scale became the Dorian, and so forth (see Fig. 14).

Fig. 14 ∧ **Fig. 15** ∨

Ironically, these were named authentic modes. The medieval equivalents of the Greek hypo scales are the plagal modes, for which the prefix 'hypo' was retained; they begin a fourth below each authentic mode (see Fig. 15). As I said in *Introducing Music*:

The differentiation of a mode was marked not only by its peculiar range of whole tones and semitones, but also by its *final*, or 'home' note, which was the lowest note of an authentic mode. Thus the final of a melody written for example in Mixolydian mode would be G. The final of the companion Hypomixolydian mode would also be G.

During the classical and romantic periods, apart from some notable exceptions, such as Beethoven's String Quartet in A minor Op. 132, modality was largely dormant, but the melodic and harmonic possibilities offered by the modal system have had a marked impact on many composers of this century. A most exquisite example is offered in Ravel's String Quartet in F, where he utilizes not only a modal scale (Phrygian mode), but also the pentatonic scale. Here are the skeletons of both scales:

A B♭ C D E F G A: Phrygian mode on A
B♭ C D F G: pentatonic scale on B♭

Ravel's unforgettable melody is quoted in Fig. 16.

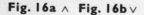

Fig. 16a ∧ **Fig. 16b** ∨

In Great Britain a notable representative is Vaughan Williams's Fantasia on a Theme by Thomas Tallis, which evokes and pays homage to an archaic world of Renaissance serenity. From Debussy to Peter Maxwell Davies the presence of modality has been – and is likely to remain with us as – an enriching and influential force.

Whole-tone scale

Infrequent use of the whole-tone scale goes back well into the nineteenth century, but its characteristic vagueness, based on six major equidistant seconds in an octave (see Fig. 17), particularly

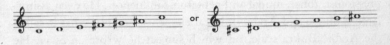

Fig. 17

suited the impressionist style. The complete lack of any reference to the main ingredients of the major–minor tonal system (that is, tonic, perfect fifth, perfect fourth, leading note) gives it its indecisive, non-tonic-oriented, drifting quality, so that it sounds like the wind passing in and out of sails. Debussy, of course, comes immediately to mind. He used it most evocatively in 'Voiles', from Bk 1 of his *Préludes* for piano (see Fig. 18).

Modéré (♪ = 88)
(Dans un rythme sans rigueur et caressant)

p très doux   *p*   *più p*

pp très doux

Fig. 18

The whole-tone scale was in vogue for a while during the first decades of this century. But because of its stylistic limitation and associations – most piano students have delighted in what could be called 'instant impressionism', playing melodies and harmonies based on the whole-tone scale – it seems to be a dead end. For this reason it is seldom in evidence in musical compositions today.

Biskra scale

'The absorption of Arabic elements in Bartók's music is not sufficiently recognized in the Bartók literature', wrote Ottó Déri in 1968 in his book *Exploring Twentieth-century Music*. Bartók had a synthetical approach to music, assimilating late-romantic, impressionist, tonal, modal and pentatonic influences. He even assimilated Balinese and Arabic musical elements, notably what is called the Arabic Biskra scale, on which subject he wrote an essay. He amalgamated all these elements into a most profound and personal twentieth-century style.

Fig. 19

What is interesting about the Biskra scale (see Fig. 19) is the interplay of major and minor thirds and the equally characteristic augmented fourth (d'–g♯'), also called the tritone. (In the Middle Ages, because of its sinister, intense sound, it was known as the 'devil in music'.) So many of Bartók's works are based on this melodic pattern that Déri went so far as to say that the Biskra scale became 'one of the trade marks of the Bartókian melodic style'. Fig. 20 is a most striking example, from the first movement of his Music for Strings, Percussion and Celesta.

Fig. 20

Serial scale

Around the early 1920s serialism was in the air. Late-romantic chromaticism, impressionism and expressionism were well-explored territories and the atonal style reached a point of no return. Few were more aware of the dilemma than Schoenberg, who felt he had created chaos with atonal chromaticism, which had to be kept at bay. After ten years of silence (1913–23), during which time he painted in an expressionist style and was free to contemplate the state of post-romantic music in Europe, he came up with one of the most revolutionary concepts in the history of music: the twelve-note system. Generally speaking, the twelve-note system can be seen as organized atonality, since Schoenberg's idea was to put order into atonal compositional thinking by arranging the twelve available chromatic notes into a set, or row or series (hence serialism), in a predetermined sequence for every composition.

Let us suppose that we want to write a melody for a solo violinist by applying this system. First we need to predetermine the note row, say:

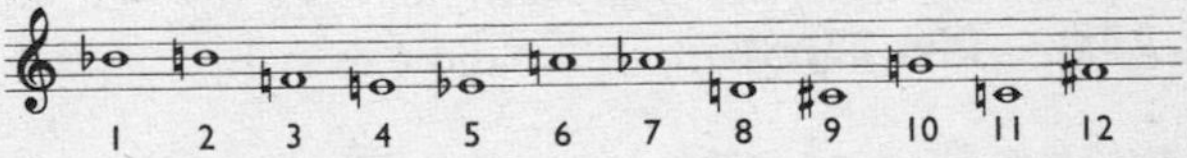

Fig. 21

The selection of the twelve notes is a most important part of the compositional process for they represent the pitches of the melody. Now let us determine, for the sake of simplicity, a rather conventional rhythmic pattern in 3/4 time (see Fig. 22). The twelve

Fig. 22

chromatic pitches have thus been shaped into a comprehensible musical statement, helped further by tempo and dynamic indications.

This, of course, is a modest, didactic illustration of the compositional principle involved in applying the twelve-note system to the construction of a serial melody. Furnished with this introduction, the reader is advised to examine and listen to the compositions of Schoenberg, Berg and Webern, whose music is largely associated with serial technique. A fine example is one of Schoenberg's early serial compositions, the Piano Suite Op. 25 (1924). Fig. 23a gives the basic set, or row; in Fig. 23b, the upper part only of the opening three bars of the Prelude, the notes of the series are numbered.

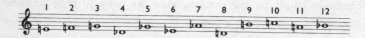

Fig. 23a ∧ **Fig. 23b** ∨

So far we have been discussing mainly the horizontal (or linear) aspects of music, such as pitch, scales and melody. Now we will turn to the vertical, that is, the harmonic aspects of twentieth-century music.

Harmony

That there is evidence of harmony in nature is proven by the fact that over a note other notes sound simultaneously with this fundamental note (see Fig. 24). These are called overtones or

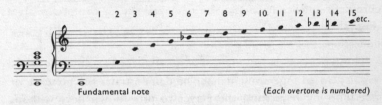

Fig. 24

harmonics. That this is so can easily be demonstrated by the following old school physics experiment: with the right hand, press down middle C on a piano without sounding it and hold on, then with the left hand play and immediately release c one octave below. As a result, middle C will sound sympathetically. Then press g' above middle C and play the c below middle C as before. The g' will now be heard to sound with great clarity. To secure a good result for an e', silently press the e' above middle C with the right hand and with the left play the C two octaves below middle C. By now you will have picked up the first four or five overtones which appear naturally in our universe, to close this statement with a Pythagorean verbal overtone.

How aware composers are of these physical elements concerning sounds can be illustrated by looking at the extract from Bartók's piano composition 'Harmonics' (*Mikrokosmos* Vol. IV No. 102) in

Fig. 25

1) ♩ Press down keys without sounding

Fig. 25. In an ingenious manner he demonstrates the presence of overtones by requesting the player to press down keys without sounding them with the left hand while the right hand plays a forceful chord which triggers the harmonics. The chord is immediately followed by a melody that reinforces the overtones over the notes silently pressed down by the left hand: an artistic indication of scientific reality.

The phenomenon of overtones or harmonics became the very basis of our harmonic system. It gave scientific foundation to the idea of sounding together as opposed to sounding in succession. Of the three basic elements of music, rhythm, melody and harmony, harmony is the youngest.

Parallel motion

Singing together in parallel octaves (see Fig. 26a), the first overtone over the fundamental note, occurs naturally when a woman and a man sing the same melody. The next step, as discussed in a tenth-

Fig. 26a

Fig. 26b

Fig. 26c
Organ voices
Principal voices

century work, *Musica enchiriadis*, was the practice of singing in parallel fourths and fifths (see Fig. 26b). This development was followed by combining voices into four parts (see Fig. 26c) by doubling the melody, the vox principalis (principal voice), and the parallel voice, vox organalis (organ voice).

Triadic thinking

By the middle of the fifteenth century the fourth partial, which is the third (see Fig. 24), was fully absorbed and combined with the fifth, thus forming a triad, the vertical combination of three sounds: that is, any note together with the third and the fifth above it (see Fig. 27).

Fig. 27
Tonic   Third   Fifth

The triad and, more particularly, triadic thinking became the foundation of Western harmony. It was the triadic system, and what evolved from it, that dominated musical theory from the Renaissance to the beginning of this century. It is for this reason that it is essential to remind ourselves, however briefly, of some of the basic concepts of tonal harmony.

Tonal harmony

The fundamental note, more often called the root, in combination with the third and fifth make up the triad, which can be either major or minor depending on whether the third is at a distance of two tones or one and a half tones from the root. In each case the fifth from the root is 'perfect'. As their names indicate, the diminished and augmented triads are formed by diminishing the fifth (in a minor triad, but in a major the third is diminished as well) by a semitone and augmenting it by a semitone (see Fig. 28).

Fig. 28
Major   Minor   Diminished Augmented

Triads can be built on any degree (note) of any scale (see Fig. 29). They are named after the degrees of the scale and can be indicated by various types of shorthand. One of the most common, especially in teaching, is to use roman numerals (I = tonic, II = supertonic, III = mediant and so on). An older and equally

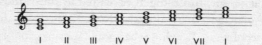
I   II   III   IV   V   VI   VII   I

Fig. 29a   Major scale

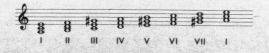
I   II   III   IV   V   VI   VII   I

Fig. 29b   Minor scale

popular method is the figured bass, whereby a chord is indicated in relation to its intervallic position over a bass. For example, in $\frac{8}{3}$ the tonic equals the root (1, which is never written), 3 is the third, 5 the fifth and 8 the octave above. According to tradition, in $\frac{5}{3}$ the root is taken for granted; the third and the fifth must be added above it. The art of playing the chords discussed above from figured bass needs understanding and practising, whether one is a Mozart or an interested layman.

We have seen that in establishing tonality as well as the home key, the tonic (I), the subdominant (IV) and the dominant (V) are of the greatest importance. It is the same with chordal thinking. Our chordal system is based on the superimposition of thirds over any given note. Fig. 30 shows how building up thirds vertically over c′, for example, creates quite complex chords.

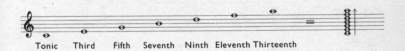

Tonic   Third   Fifth   Seventh   Ninth   Eleventh Thirteenth

Fig. 30

Cadences

As in language, so in music it is necessary to punctuate. In tonal music this is achieved by using cadences. There are four basic cadences (see Fig. 31), whose harmonic progression is defined under the following names: perfect (V–I); plagal (IV–I); imperfect (any chord to V); interrupted (V–VI). Both the perfect and the plagal cadences act as the equivalent of a full stop. The imperfect cadence, as its name suggests, leaves things unfinished, hanging in the air. When an interrupted cadence appears at the end of a phrase it gives an unexpected, sudden stop effect, after which there is a strong feeling that something must follow in order to resolve the tension created. The interruption is created by the dominant moving to the submediant rather than, as expected, the tonic. In a sense it delays the home-coming.

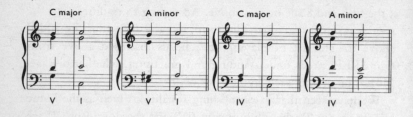

Fig. 31

Primary and secondary triads

In tonal music, however complex the harmonic thinking, the triads built on I, IV and V are foundation stones both harmonically and structurally. For this reason the tonic, subdominant and dominant triads are called primary triads. The rest (II, III, VI, VII) are referred to as secondary triads.

In 1722 Bach completed his first set of preludes and fugues, entitled *Das wohltemperirte Clavier*, in which he set out to demonstrate the technical advantages gained by the equal temperament system. That same year another notable work, by the French composer Jean-Philippe Rameau, appeared in Paris. In his treatise (*Traité de l'harmonie*) Rameau conceptualized what was partly in practice already, that chords can be inverted (rotated) so that the third or fifth takes the lowest part (see Fig. 32). Moreover, he

Fig. 32   Root position   First inversion   Second inversion

evolved the theory of chord progression, which explains the order in which chords can move from one to another:

  I (Tonic) can be followed by any chord.
 II (Supertonic) can be followed by V, III, IV, VI or VII.
III (Mediant) can be followed by VI, IV, II, V.
IV (Subdominant) can be followed by V, I, VI, II, VII, III.
 V (Dominant) can be followed by I, VI, III, IV.
VI (Submediant) can be followed by II, V, IV, III.
VII (Seventh) can be followed by I, VI, III, V.

Thus Rameau, a true son of the Age of Reason, presented us with a tonal theory which summed up scientifically the ways chords can be organized. Although his theories met with plenty of critical objections, especially his theory of inversion, his influence, to this day, is considerable.

The weakening of tonality

After about three hundred years of domination and evolution tonal music reached its apotheosis during the second half of the nineteenth century. But, as has often happened in the history of the arts, when the style arrived at its peak, the new was already undermining the very foundations of the old. Some of the instigators of the new, such as Wagner and Liszt, were among the most romantic composers. The chromatic world of Liszt reached a point where tonality was not only substantially weakened but, in some of his later works, abandoned altogether.

Let us look now at some high-romantic chromaticism in which tonality is obscured and delayed. One of the best-known examples is Wagner's Prelude to *Tristan und Isolde* (see Fig. 33). As no key signature is given and the starting note is a, we might as well

Fig. 33

assume that the tonality is A minor. In bar 2 and at the beginning of bar 3 we encounter chromaticism which obscures the sense of tonality, but the dominant seventh chord of A minor is clear at bar 3, when the chromatic a#' finally leads to a momentary rest on b'. The chromatically reached b' is the fifth of the dominant seventh chord (E G# B D; Wagner's spacing is e g# d' b'). This passage is sequentially repeated, but now the chromatic alterations lead to the dominant seventh of C major. In fact, the music stays in the key of A minor for forty-three bars, though that key is only arrived at in passing on a few occasions. Further scrutiny of the same seven bars reveals the striking presence of diminished and augmented intervals (for example bar 2: f–b, d#'–a'; bar 3: d♮'–

a♯′; bar 6: a♭–d′, f♯′–c″). In Fig. 34, again from Wagner's *Tristan*, the density of chromatic notes is such that within the short passage all twelve chromatic notes of the scale are utilized, making it almost like a note row (see p. 15).

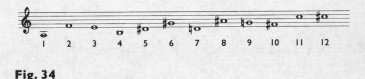

Fig. 34

The opening of Liszt's *Faust Symphony* offers not only a note-row effect, but also a powerful series of augmented triads (see Fig. 35). On account of this passage, it would be hard to tell that the movement is in C minor.

Fig. 35

One of Liszt's late piano works, *Nuages gris* (1881), carries a key signature of two flats, indicating the tonality of G minor. The piece is dominated by the presence of augmented and diminished intervals and chords. Over a tremolo on B♭′ (see Fig. 36a) a chromatically descending chord progression in the first half is balanced by a descending chromatic passage in the last bars (see Fig. 36b). The work ends not in the home key of G minor but on an a. The whole composition is remarkable for its impressionistic atmosphere, created well before Debussy evoked nature with his

Fig. 36a ∧   **Fig. 36b** ∨

sound tableaux. The last two chords are of particular interest as they display ingenious harmonic thinking. The orthodox resolution to the tonic of G minor is there in the upper part: f♯'' (leading note) moves to g'' (tonic). The third is raised to b♮'. This is an old technique, known as the Picardy third, whereby a piece of music in a minor key ends with a major third. In the lower part, however, the a and e♭' give a dissonant, unresolved, floating quality appropriate to the title of the composition. (Note the diminished fifth; a–e♭', and the augmented fifth, e♭'–b♮'.) Relatively complex as this last chord is, its foundation is triadic. By superimposing thirds from G we have the following choice of notes: G B♮ D F♯ A C E♭. Naming these notes according to their intervallic (or numerical) distance, we have the tonic, third, fifth, major seventh, major ninth, eleventh, and minor thirteenth. This series contains the notes of Liszt's chord, except the fifth, seventh and eleventh, the least important notes in defining the character of a tonic thirteenth (the sharpened seventh had appeared in the previous bar). Using the triadic system and even by applying Rameau's inversion theory, we can conclude that this chord is the fourth inversion of a tonic thirteenth. There are other possible explanations, but that is beside the point. What we have demonstrated here is that the triadic harmonic idioms, including Rameau's vexed inversion theory, can still help us to come closer to an understanding of what is going on harmonically in a composition which is already stretching the outer limits of traditional harmonic thinking.

Consonance and dissonance

It was Helmholtz who in the nineteenth century defined the distinction between consonance and dissonance by demonstrating that an interval was consonant when the two notes producing it shared overtones. The more overtones they share, the more consonant they are; the fewer they share, the more dissonant. The same principle can be applied to chords. Consonant intervals are the octave, perfect fourth, perfect fifth, third and sixth; dissonant intervals are the second, seventh, ninth and so on. Although the use of consonance and dissonance has fluctuated considerably in the history of music, it is fair to say that during its long evolution music has shown a gradual absorption of dissonance and that from the nineteenth century dissonance has gradually become more common than consonance. It is in this context that Schoenberg spoke about the 'emancipation of dissonance'.

Slow, vague, indecisive

Fig. 37

Tonal alienation

The Prelude for piano by Skryabin in Fig. 37 is to be played slowly, vaguely and indecisively. The chromatic chords wander away from and yet are still within sight of tonality. The ambiguity, as in Liszt, is further emphasized by the use of augmented triads and the augmented fourth. The introduction of triplets creates a metric oscillation, while the simultaneous sounding of A major and minor (A E C♮ A C♯) gives a dissonant twist to the tonality of A, which is reached at the end via a tritonal chord that acts as a quasi-plagal cadence. In spite of the tonality of A, however, one does not feel 'at home'. We could speak here of 'tonal alienation' in the sense that because we have been away for so long, the feeling of stability is lost to such an extent that even the home key is seen as just another potential departure point, like all the others. The result is suspense rather than rest, unsettledness instead of reassurance. For most music lovers, this is probably one of the hardest aspects of twentieth-century music to come to terms with.

Superimposing fourths

In his search for a new harmonic language Skryabin touched upon the idea of serialism. He found that a single set of notes may be the foundation of both the melodic and harmonic material of a composition. Accordingly, he worked out a chord based on fourths, which became his 'mystic' chord: D G C F♯ B♭ E. This served as the basis of his *Prometheus*. It is interesting to observe that the mystic chord dispenses with triadic thinking in favour of a combination of perfect, diminished and augmented fourths.

Richard Strauss is now seen as a post-Wagnerian romantic composer who, by virtue of his life span (1864–1949), may conveniently be classed as a transitory figure between late romanticism and the modern era. Yet at the height of his creative power he was esteemed as the modern composer *par excellence*, and exercised a major influence on several of his contemporary composers.

Apart from the brilliance of his orchestration, to be discussed in Chapter Four, what were those modern characteristics, blended into his overall romantic style, which could inspire such composers as Bartók? The answer is, of course, complex; here, though, are some strikingly modernistic features of his music:

(a) frequent use of tritones (augmented fourth, diminished fifth)

Fig. 38 *Elektra*

(b) polytonality

Fig. 39 'Für funfzehn Pfennige'

(c) polyrhythm

Fig. 40 *Salome*

(d) structured twelve-note chromaticism within tonality

Fig. 41 *Also sprach Zarathustra*

One could list more characteristics, but here it is sufficient to draw attention to the ones that seem to have preoccupied several composers around the years 1880–1915, among whom Strauss was prominent.

Breaking away from Austro-German musical hegemony

Nineteenth-century romanticism in music was largely dominated by the Austro-German musical tradition, and above all by the sonata-structured symphonic tradition. One of the most striking achievements of Debussy was to free himself from that domination and to reclaim a leading role for French music, of which he became the foremost exponent. He even came to refer to himself as 'musicien français'. Although a Wagnerite to begin with, he quickly moved away from the temptations of Wagner's musical Venusberg. He found his voice by breaking with convention, turning to the past, to folk music, to the Mediterranean world and the Far East as well as to Modest Mussorgsky, whose liberating, free-minded influence he was always ready to acknowledge. Debussy's harmonic thinking was the most novel aspect of his music. He too has greatly contributed to the gradual erosion of the major–minor key system, instead of which he used modality and pentatonic and whole-tone scales. Moreover, he discarded textbook rules and regulations and worked with chords instinctively, considering nothing but their individual sound values. The deterministic gravitational pull of functional, traditional harmony, with its rational resolutions, was replaced by sensual, non-directional, unresolved, drifting harmony. Consecutive fifths, which were largely forbidden in traditional harmony, became one of his most frequent progressions (see Fig. 42, from 'Doctor Gradus ad Parnassum'). Similarly, the medieval parallel organum gained renowned significance in his musical vocabulary (see Fig. 43, from 'La Cathédrale engloutie', *Préludes* Bk 1) and ninth chords (for example, G B D F A) became one of his trade marks (see Fig. 44, from 'Canope', *Préludes* Bk 2). Ninth chords came to be associated not only with Debussy, but also with other French composers, notably Ravel. Fig. 45 is a splendid example, taken from Ravel's *Pavane pour une infante défunte*.

Très animé

Fig. 42

Fig. 43a ∧ **Fig. 43b** ∨

Fig. 44 ∧ **Fig. 45** ∨

Another Debussyism, which we have already touched upon (see p. 13), is the use of the whole-tone scale. The lack of semitones in the quotation from *Pelléas et Mélisande* in Fig. 46 gives a sense of indefiniteness.

Fig. 46

Added notes chords

Debussy often added to a chord a note a sixth above its root (for example C E G A), something much loved by jazz players, or any unrelated note, just for the sake of the atmospheric, spicy effects. In the extract from the 'Golliwogg's Cake Walk' in Fig. 47 the f (notably a ninth above the root) is played against the E♭ major chord.

Fig. 47

These were a few basic examples of the so-called impressionist harmonic vocabulary, which has greatly contributed to bringing about a change in our musical thinking.

Modern tonality

As we have seen, for many composers freedom in harmonic thinking did not mean a complete abandonment of tonality. They worked around, near, on or with it, but not without it. Until he turned to serialism in the 1950s, Stravinsky's harmonic thinking, for instance, was tonal, albeit unorthodox.

Bitonality

In *Petrushka* we find the superimposition of two tonalities, C major and F♯ major (see Fig. 48). This procedure, called bitonality, is common in the works belonging to both the Russian and the neoclassical periods of Stravinsky. One of his most famous uses of

Fig. 48 ∧   **Fig. 49** ∨

bitonality is the opening of the 'Dance of the Youths and Maidens' in *The Rite of Spring*, where the chords of F♭ and E♭ are superimposed in a most elemental manner (see Fig. 49).

Here one is confronted with the evocation of an Asiatic past with an immediacy and intensity similar to that found in Picasso's African-influenced painting *Les Demoiselles d'Avignon*. The harmony is subservient to the rhythm as it is used for its dissonant, percussive timbre enhancing the overall neo-primitive, ritualistic dance effect. The idea of dual harmonic thinking was, of course, practised by other composers, such as Bartók. But perhaps the most consistent user of polytonality was Milhaud, who, together with the other members of Les Six, reacted against the sensuousness of Debussy. In order to avoid musical impressionism, Milhaud turned to harsh dissonance, often jazz-influenced rhythm and sharp colours in orchestration. Polytonality particularly suited his style. In his Sonata for flute, oboe, clarinet and piano F major and C major, then F♯ major and C major, are played at the same time; in his Piano Concerto No. 3 the orchestra is in D major while the solo piano part is in E major. Charles Ives, who seems to have anticipated – or, at least, paralleled – most modern European developments in music in far-away Newfoundland, was also fond of polytonality, as his simultaneous setting in G minor and C major of Psalm 67 illustrates (see Fig. 50).

Fig. 50

So far we have seen that in triadic harmony one can multiply harmonic possibilities by adding thirds over a note. In traditional music the use of thirds and sevenths in all their manifestations was the daily bread of harmonic expression. As the tonal system evolved and expanded, chords of ninths, elevenths, thirteenths and beyond were incorporated into the harmonic vocabulary of many modern composers. New possibilities opened up by building chords not on thirds but on fourths. This quartal harmony was utilized by several twentieth-century composers, notably Skryabin, Bartók, Berg, Hindemith, Stravinsky and Schoenberg. So was the added note technique, as we saw when discussing Debussy's techniques (p. 35). Now we turn to one of the most dissonant ways of building chords, the secondal method.

Secondal harmony

This is formed by playing together two or more notes which are a major or minor second from each other. In Fig. 51a they are in closed position; they can also be spaced in open position (Fig. 51b) and in inversion (Fig. 51c).

Fig. 51

Most twentieth-century composers have used secondal harmony in one way or another, some, such as Cowell, Ives and Bartók, more often than others. The extracts from Debussy's 'Feux d'artifice' (*Préludes* Bk 2) in Fig. 52a and Bartók's 'Major Seconds Broken and Together' (*Mikrokosmos* Vol. V No. 132) in Fig. 52b demonstrate its practical use.

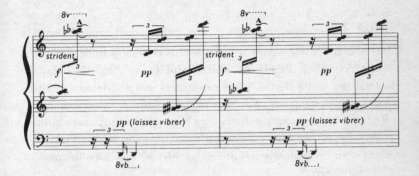

Fig. 52a

Adagio, ♩. = ca 56 - 52

Fig. 52b

Clusters

The transition from secondal harmony to clusters is quite natural, for the degree of density in which seconds are piled up defines clusteral thinking. Bartók's use of clusters in his 'Melody in the Mist' (*Mikrokosmos* Vol. IV No. 107) is relatively simple as it is still related to secondal harmony (see Fig. 53). Ives's clusters in his *Concord Sonata* (see Fig. 54) confront us, however, with a maze of sounds with considerable notational problems, as will be discussed in Chapter Two.

Tranquillo, ♩. = 46

Fig. 53

Fig. 54

Free atonal, dodecaphonic and partial serialism

We have already touched upon some aspects of atonality and serialism, and will now venture a step further. When approaching non-tonality-oriented music, it is prudent to distinguish, in their chronological appearance, between free atonality, dodecaphonic (twelve-note serial system) and partial serialism. As we have seen, atonality discards traditional tonal gravitation, but does not replace it with a coherent system. Dodecaphony, on the other hand, offers a system: organized or systematic atonality. In partial serialism composers, while applying the system, do not feel obliged to utilize all twelve chromatic notes of the dodecaphonic system, but instead restrict themselves to fewer chromatic notes, say five or six. Let us discuss these now in turn.

Free atonality

Atonal music grew out of the extreme chromaticism of the late-romantic period. One could postulate that during the early twentieth century atonal music was the ultimate conclusion. Indeed, it seems to have represented the chaotic dead end of chromatic thinking, which is how Schoenberg himself anxiously saw it. The last of his Six Little Piano Pieces Op. 19 (see Fig. 55) is a piece of extreme brevity which cannot be explained in terms of traditional tonal analysis. There is no tonic, though the long, held and repeated a′ and the similarly treated c′, as well as the fact that the last note drops down a semitone from the opening a♮′ to the final A♭′ in the bass, seem to indicate a chromatic preoccupation *around* A and C. The characteristic 'septimal thinking' (as Stuckenschmidt put it in his book *Neue Musik*) of twentieth-century composers is evident throughout the whole piece. So is the superimposition of fourths (f♯″–b″, g–c′–f′, c′–f′–b♭′) and also whole tones (bars 5–6). These are, of course, immediate and obvious pickings. Further

Sehr langsam (♩)

Fig. 55

investigation reveals that in between the held chords, which give a quasi-static quality to the music, a motif-like figure is imbedded (f#'–g'–f#'). The downward falling figure reappears at bars 5–6 (g#–f#), bar 7, where the fall is a minor third (f#–eb), and bar 8, where both the downward and upward moves are combined (f#–g; eb'–eb'). Cadential points may be defined at bars 4, 6, 7, 8 and 9. The greatest intensity of movement appears at bars 7 and 8. It is in bar 7 that the music is at its loudest (*p*), in a piece where the dynamic ranges are *p*, *pp*, *ppp*, *pppp*. At bar 9 the held chords of the opening bars are reintroduced, but instead of starting with an upbeat they begin on the strong beat. The second strong beat entry of the left-hand chord in bar 1 is now on the second, weak beat of bar 9. On the last beat two quavers, B♭ and A♭′, are played at a distance of a major ninth, as if echoing the drop of a minor sixteenth in bar 7. The note value of the upbeat start, contrary to usual practice, is not deducted from the last bar.

As far as the underlying structure is concerned, it is a matter of opinion as to whether the breaking up of this piece into meaningful segments leads the analyst to six, seven or another number of units. A reader has done well if he or she has absorbed the following:

A held chords: bars 1–6
B rising and falling motifs: bars 3–4–5–6
C agitated density and combined material of A and B (for example f♯′–g′ in bar 3 reappears at bar 7, c♯–d, and at bar 8, f♯–g): bars 7–8
A return of held chords: bar 9

Dodecaphony

Dodecaphonic technique, in which twelve notes are 'related to one another', is basically a contrapuntal device. As the tonal centre, and therefore the traditional harmonic hierarchy, is discarded, harmony is secondary in importance to the linear (horizontal) and motivic domination of the series, which predetermines both the horizontal and vertical aspects of the composition. We have already seen how a twelve-note series, or twelve-note row, as it is sometimes referred to, can be constructed and how a melody, or, rather, a musical statement, can be built on it (see pp. 15–16). Now we will look at both the horizontal and the vertical, that is, the harmonic implications of the dodecaphonic system. It

could be argued that one of the most lyrical and immediately
attractive dodecaphonic compositions in the repertory is Berg's
Violin Concerto, not only because of his lyrical temperament,
but also because of his ingenious fusion of tonal elements into the
dodecaphonic system. This is made clear by the way he structured
the series on which the concerto is based (see Fig. 56). The minor–
major–minor–major triadic chain is rounded off by a partial

Fig. 56

whole-tone scale. These whole tones (notes 9–12) are not, as they
might seem, an impressionistic reference to Debussy, but a direct
quotation from Bach's chorale *Es ist genug*. By singling out from
the series notes 1, 3, 5 and 7 we find the open strings of the violin:
g d′ a′ e″. This set of fifths is used at the introductory opening of
the concerto (see Fig. 57).

The composition is dodecaphonic, but has an inbuilt ambivalent
vacillation between G minor and B♭ major. In the piano reduction
of the score in Fig. 58 the reader can study how the vertical
implication of the original series is utilized. At the end of this
passage the solo violin introduces the complete series in its original
(see Fig. 59).

At this point we may examine some of the many ways in
which the series can be manipulated. The ideas of playing a
passage backwards or of inverting it and so forth are, of course,
not new. They belong to the Western contrapuntal tradition,
which has been incorporated into the serial system. For the sake of
simplicity, consider the first six notes of Berg's series: g♮ b♭ d♮′ f♯′
a♮′ c♮″. These are in their original positions. By playing them

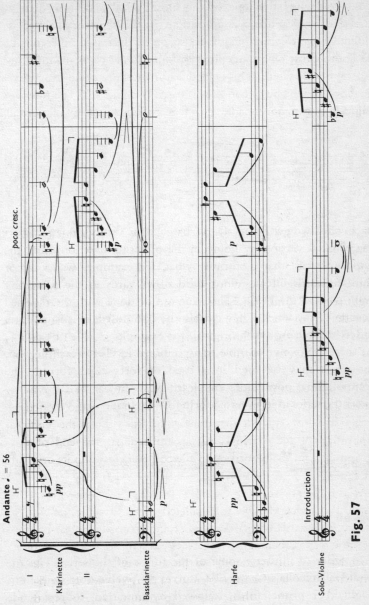

Fig. 57

Fig. 58 ∧   **Fig. 59** ∨

backwards we get c♮'' a♮' f♯' d♮' b♭ g♮'. It is also possible to invert the original version by going in the opposite direction using the same intervals, that is, turning what, for example, was a minor third upwards into a minor third downwards in the following way: g♮ e♮ c♮ A♭ F♮ D♮. The same can be done with the reversed version of the series. They can also be transposed, that is, put at a different pitch from the original, for example: c♮ e♭ g♮ b♭ d♮' f♮'. As there are twelve possible transpositional levels for each version, the series may be used in a total of forty-eight forms. The compositional possibilities are clearly vast. At bar 24 Berg introduces the series in its inverted form (see Fig. 60).

Fig. 60

In order to illustrate some of the forms of the series, Fig. 61, from Dallapicolla's *Goethe Lieder*, gives the twelve-note series in its original, or prime, form, followed by imitation, its retrograde

Fig. 61

inversion and its retrograde, together with the first line of the
song 'Die Sonne kommt!' in its original primary position.

Partial serialism

In partial serialism composers choose not to stick to twelve notes,
but to use more or fewer notes for their series. Some outstanding
examples are Schoenberg's Five Piano Pieces Op. 23 No. 2 (nine-
note series), Stravinsky's *In memoriam Dylan Thomas* (five-note
series) and Schoenberg's Serenade Op. 24 (fourteen-note series).
Fig. 62a is the series Stravinsky used in *In memoriam Dylan
Thomas*; the piece's opening is quoted in Fig. 62b.

Fig. 62a ∧   **Fig. 62b** ∨

Total serialism

From Webern onwards several composers felt that the application
of old-style rhythm, dynamics and instrumentation was somewhat
incongruous in the context of the new serial compositional style.
Dissatisfaction with this state of affairs eventually led to the
writing of music which was serial not only in pitch, but also in
other matters musical. Webern, Messiaen, Babbitt, Boulez and
Stockhausen were in the forefront of thinking in terms of serializ-

ing elements other than pitch, above all rhythm and dynamics. Messiaen and Boulez even serialized modes of attack. In his *Structures* for two pianos Boulez, influenced by Messiaen's *Mode de valeurs et d'intensités* for piano, worked out an ingenious grading of dynamics based on the twelve numbers of the series:

1	2	3	4	5	6	7	8	9	10	11	12
pppp	*ppp*	*pp*	*p*	*quasi p*	*mp*	*mf*	*quasi f*	*f*	*ff*	*fff*	*ffff*

Extending the dodecaphonic method to other parameters of a musical work enabled composers to predetermine the order of virtually every aspect. This may seem to many music lovers to be over-mathematical, to the point of being impersonal and mechanical. We should remember, however, that similar accusations could easily be expressed with regard to compositional methods of earlier periods and that a genius will always transcend the limitations of any system. For instance, the fact that Berg's opera *Lulu* is based on the dodecaphonic system should not distract us from its overall dramatic impact. Arranging the notes of the series (see Fig. 63a) vertically into four chords creates the theme of Lulu's portrait (see Fig. 63b); playing these notes linearly, across the upper then middle and the lower parts (see Fig. 63c), produces another

Fig. 63a ∧   Fig. 63b >

Fig. 63c

important Lulu theme. It is indeed crafty, but it is also inspired. In Berg's hands these technical elements served in the structuring and unfolding of a great twentieth-century opera.

It is true that the numerically inclined rigour called for in serialism, total or otherwise, introduced into compositional art a markedly scientific attitude. From about the middle of this century there has been an increasing tendency towards musical developments, such as electronic music, which have brought forth a vogue for a new type of musician: the composer-performer-scientist. Several composers – Boulez, Stockhausen, Babbitt and Xenakis, to mention a few outstanding examples – have strong mathematical interests or scientific training. One of the great theoreticians of our century, Joseph Schillinger, in his fascinating book *The Mathematical Basis of the Arts* wrote: 'If art implies selectivity, skill and organization, ascertainable principles must underlie it. Once such principles are discovered and formulated, works of art may be produced by scientific synthesis.' Then he goes on to question the very freedom of the artist in connection with self-expression, as all artists are by the nature of things restricted and influenced by cultural, geographical and historical boundaries. His Utopian conclusion is that the 'key to real freedom and emancipation from local dependence is through scientific method'. With that view, no wonder that, as early as 1932, he wrote about 'Electricity, a liberator of music!'

Chance music

The opposite of exercising total control is to leave more or less everything to chance. After total determinacy, total indeterminacy. Cage, one of the main protagonists in this compositional style from 1950 onwards, was to write music in two distinctive ways based on chance or aleatory techniques (from the Latin *alea* = dice, that is, playing with dice selection). In the first method the composer virtually throws dice in order to arrive at haphazard indications for manipulating sound material; if there are no dice around, the tossing of coins will do (as, for example, in Cage's *Music of Changes*). In the second the composer gives a basic outline of his or her intentions, and the rest, the details, are to be performed according to the player's personal choice (as in Morton Feldman's *Last Pieces*). Cage based his theory on the classical Chinese I Ching (Book of changes). But Xenakis, an engineer by training, is influenced by mathematics and, more specifically, the probability theory as applied to games, something which goes back to the time of Pascal and Fermat, who became involved in working out mathematical problems sent to them by a gambler.

It was Zen-influenced, non-intentional thinking which largely motivated Cage to write aleatory music. One of his most striking examples of chance 'composition' is for twelve radios, *Imaginary Landscape No. 4*. This enabled him to generate, at any time, unpredictable sound effects by tuning in to different radio stations at random. In his book *Silence* he explains:

It is thus possible to make a musical composition the continuity of which is free of individual taste and memory (psychology) and also of the literature and 'traditions' of the art. The sounds enter the time-space centred within themselves, unimpeded by service to any abstraction, their 360 degree of circumference free for an infinite play of interpretation. Value judgements are not in the nature of this work as regards either composition, performance or listening . . . A 'mistake' is beside the point, for once anything happens it authentically is.

The ultimate step in this direction has to be his *4' 33"*, where the composition is based on the sounds a silent audience is likely to be able to hear during that specified period of silence. It would be a grave mistake, however, to think of Cage as something of an irreverent clown, though clowning is part of his style; he is out to shock us. It is his obsessive preoccupation with sounds – or, rather, the integrity of sound as sound irrespective of the composer, performer and listener – which leads him to his most illuminating thoughts. He is one of the great experimentalists of our century, and without him our musical perception, as well as our awareness of sound (not necessarily the same thing), would have been all the poorer. The reader is referred to his Concerto for piano and orchestra on the one hand and *Imaginary Landscape No. 4* on the other to illustrate this point.

Counterpoint

The term 'counterpoint' (derived from the Latin *punctus contra punctum* = note against note) is technically synonymous with 'polyphony' (Greek *poly* = many). It denotes a compositional method in which the independent interests of two or more melodic lines are maintained in combination with each other. Some contemporary composers, such as Babbitt, Boulez and Ligeti, prefer the term 'polyphony', and use it to describe their individual forms of counterpoint.

Although it is advisable to approach with caution the common belief that in the nineteenth century music was largely homophonic and that counterpoint was dormant, it is certainly true that in comparison with the baroque period nineteenth-century music showed markedly less preoccupation with counterpoint. It is therefore justifiable to speak of a revival of contrapuntal thinking during the twentieth century. We have already commented upon the fact that serialism is based on polyphonic thinking. So, moreover, was the neoclassical movement, which largely meant a return to baroque contrapuntal practices as exemplified by Bach. Indeed, one of the neoclassicists' slogans was 'Back to Bach'. This being so, before turning to some twentieth-century contrapuntal works, we will first look at one characteristic example by Bach in order to see what fascinated and still fascinates twentieth-century composers studying his music and what they are trying to emulate and reinterpret within the context of our own century.

Fig. 64a gives the first two bars of Bach's Prelude No. XX in A minor from the second book of the '48'. The first bar contains the

two melodic elements of the piece, which consists of thirty-two
bars in all. Both melodic lines are chromatic and, as the second bar
illustrates, interchangeable: what was in the top line in bar 1 is in
the bottom line in bar 2 and vice versa. By looking more closely
we find that there is a relationship between the downwards-moving
lower voice and the upper voice: c″ b′ bb′ a′ g#′. After reaching
the dominant of A minor at bar 16, the exact halfway point, Bach
inverts the two motifs, as well as reversing the entries of the voices
(see Fig. 64b): the inverted lower part is in the upper part, while
the inverted upper part is now in the lower part, thus inverting
the roles of the opening two bars. In a nutshell, this Prelude
represents contrapuntal thinking of the utmost concentration in

Fig. 64a ∧ Fig. 64b ∨

which linear independence and thematic and harmonic elements are synchronized with great rigour.

Simple two-part writing

The renewed interest in contrapuntal textures during this century gained expression in the cultivation of compositional procedures which were much in favour during the baroque period, such as thematic imitation, canon and fugue. We will now examine these in the works of some twentieth-century composers, beginning with an example of non-imitative two-part writing from Stravinsky's folk-influenced *Petrushka*. Fig. 65a shows only the two outer parts, moving in contrary motion and each maintaining its own melodic independence; Fig. 65b includes the harmonic filling, with all parts in parallel motion.

Fig. 65a ∧ **Fig. 65b** ∨

Simple four-part writing

The chorale from *The Soldier's Tale* quoted in Fig. 66 looks like a Bach chorale, but sounds quite different owing to the so-called wrong-note technique Stravinsky used to give a parodying twist to both its melodic and harmonic aspects.

Fig. 66

Mixed polyphonic texture

In the second movement of Bartók's Third Piano Concerto we find that the imitative entries of the strings (see Fig. 67a) lead to the entry of the soloist, who plays a chorale-like theme (see Fig. 67b). In the third part of the movement the chorale theme is given to the wind section while the pianist plays a free imitative two-part invention (see Fig. 67c). It is a moving example of Bartók's profound absorption of Bach's polyphonic thinking.

Fig. 67a

Fig. 67b ∧ Fig. 67c ∨

Multiple thematic imitation

Multiple thematic imitation occurs when two or more musical ideas (motifs) are combined together in imitation, as we saw with Bach (Fig. 64). A straightforward modern example to illustrate the essence of this technique is to be found in Schoenberg's Three Piano Pieces Op. 11 No. 1, quoted in Fig. 68. The asterisked motifs show how Schoenberg maintains unity and coherence by contrapuntal means. That the piece is freely atonal and therefore lacks the harmonic cohesion offered by tonal harmony is compensated for by polyphonic cross-references.

Fig. 68

The technique of inversion — that is, the swapping of voices, whereby the lower voice becomes the higher and vice versa — is also known as double counterpoint. Although the term was originally associated with tonal music, it is equally applicable to music in which the tonal centre is either blurred or virtually discarded. When three or four voices are similarly interchangeable, musicians speak of triple and quadruple counterpoints.

Canon

The practice of writing in canon (Latin *canon* = rule), where a melodic part is shortly followed by another using the same melodic idea and so on with three, four or more voices, goes well back into the Middle Ages. A fine example is 'Summer is icumen in', dating from the mid thirteenth century; better-known examples are 'Three Blind Mice' and 'Frère Jacques'. In twentieth-century music the vogue for canonic writing corresponds to the 'Back to Bach' movement, as Bach was one of the great masters of every form of polyphonic writing, including canon (see, for example, the Goldberg Variations). Polyphonic texture was used by the neoclassicists Reger, Busoni, Stravinsky, Bartók and Hindemith, as well as by such serialists as Schoenberg and, above all, Webern, whose music is dominated by canonic thinking. Fig. 69 gives the first five bars of Webern's Concerto for nine instruments Op. 24 (flute, oboe, clarinet, horn, trumpet, trombone, violin, viola and piano). This is a complex passage, made difficult by the

* sound as written

Fig. 69

use of inversion, augmentation and subtle rhythmic drifts. The canonic motif, based on the first three notes of the set (b♮ b♭ d♮'), is in a state of constant flux. The set itself (see Fig. 70) is built on contrapuntal and durational variations of the first three notes.

Original   Retrograde inversion   Retrograde   Inversion

Fig. 70

It was this concentrated, ascetic devotion to sound and compositional craft, among other things, that made Stravinsky write in 1955, ten years after the tragic death of Webern:

The 15th of September 1945, the day of Anton Webern's death, should be a day of mourning for any receptive musician. We must hail not only this great composer but also a real hero. Doomed to failure in a deaf world of ignorance and indifference he inexorably kept on cutting out his diamonds, his dazzling diamonds, the mines of which he had such perfect knowledge.

There are many canonic devices with which the composer can display his or her technical skill. The most frequently used are canon by inversion (when the melody is inverted); crab or retrograde canon (when the melody is imitated, but by playing it backwards); augmented or diminished canon (the time values of the imitation are either longer or shorter than those of the original motif). However mechanical these may seem, they call for great technical and musical ingenuity, and it is the success of the resulting sound that distinguishes the master.

Fugue

Bach was one of the greatest exponents of fugal composition. He left us, in addition to his organ music, the Goldberg Variations

and the '48', such monumental essays in sound as the *Musical
Offering* and *The Art of Fugue,* in which contrapuntal writing in
general and the fugue in particular are explored to the limit, so it
is natural that we should turn to him again for illuminating
guidance. The fugue (Latin *fuga* = flight) is among the most
elaborate manifestations of polyphonic writing. Its unfolding,
imitative texture may contain many of the contrapuntal ideas
discussed above; they may be restricted to one fugue or worked
out in a set of several fugues, as is the case with Bach's *Art of
Fugue.* The opening fugue subject is explored in its original,
inverted, augmented, diminished and retrograde versions (see Fig.
71).

Fig. 71a

Fig. 71b ∧ **Fig. 71c** ∨

Fig. 71d ∧ **Fig. 71e** ∨

Fugues, apart from the academic kind, do not fit easily into a stereotyped pattern; the more fugues that are written, the greater the number of possible overall structures. Yet there are certain characteristic features which are relevant to this day.

Subject A fugue is based on a pertinent melodic theme, or subject, which is stated alone at the beginning.

Answer This is the imitation of the subject.

Counter-subject The melodic line which appears simultaneously with the answer is known as the counter-subject.

Voices There are fugues with two, five and even six parts, or voices, but the majority are for three or four voices.

Episode The episode is a contrasting passage between the subject and its reiteration.

Exposition This is the opening of a fugue, and the part in which all the voices enter.

Middle section The middle section follows the exposition and it is here that one or more episodes are introduced with further contrapuntal development. In tonal music these are in related keys. In twentieth-century music, however, there are usually free entries of the subject at various pitches. In serial music the fugue would, of course, follow dodecaphonic rules.

Final section As the name indicates, at this point the fugue returns to its original pitch, leading to the culmination of the whole fugue.

Fughetta A fughetta (meaning 'small fugue') is a short or 'light' fugue.

Fugato A passage in a larger work (for example the exposition) which is written in the style of a fugue but is not developed much further is called fugato; it is thus distinguished from a real fugue.

Other elements associated with fugue include the pedal, or pedal point, an elongated or repeated bass note over which the upper part moves, and stretto, which occurs when the answer enters before the subject is finished, creating an overlapping and urging effect.

The above list does not cover every aspect of fugal writing. The point has been to give the reader a basic understanding of fugal procedure so that its complexities, whether past or present, can be appreciated. Fig. 72 is the exposition of Fugue No. VI in D minor from the second book of Bach's '48'. The fugue consists of twenty-seven bars in all, but in that short space Bach packs in three episodes; a canon between the bass and treble voices (bars 19–21); stretto in original form (bars 14–15); stretto in inversion (bars 17–18).

During 1932–3 Webern gave a series of lectures, later published under the title *The Path to the New Music*, in which the name of Bach figures prominently: 'For everything happens in Bach.' In connection with Bach's *Art of Fugue* he observed: 'All these fugues are based on *one* single theme, which is constantly transformed: a thick book of musical ideas whose whole content arises from a single idea! What does all this mean? The desire for maximum

Fig. 72

unity. Everything is derived from one basic idea, from the one fugue-theme! Everything is "thematic".' The relationship between Bach and modernism in music is revealed by the enthusiastic observations of Webern. The search for total unity, for the unfolding of musical potential in a form of 'perpetual variation' in which everything is related to a central idea, was Webern's own quest, and in Bach he found a precursor.

Let us now turn to direct musical references. Bach himself laid down the foundation of a tradition when he set to music the letters of his name B–A–C–H (the German names of the notes B♭ A C B♮) in the last incomplete fugue of *The Art of Fugue*. Since then several composers have followed suit, including Webern, who structured his series for the String Quartet Op. 28 on B–A–C–H in a most concentrated manner (see Fig. 73). A close

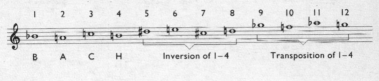

Fig. 73

look at the series will reveal that Webern used the first four notes, the B–A–C–H motif, in such a way that all the remaining notes derived from it: d♯″ e♮″ c♯″ d♮″ is the inversion of the motif and the last four notes are the transposition of the original motif to g♭″ f♮″ a♭″ g♮″. The three movements during which the motif is developed in canonic, variation and fugato styles (see the middle section of the third movement) show how far Webern has gone in achieving his concept of being able to develop everything from one principal idea. His search for roots led him to Bach and beyond to the northern Renaissance masters. Fig. 74 illustrates the intricate ways in which Webern uses the B–A–C–H motif.

Just over a year before the completion of Webern's String Quartet Op. 28 in 1938 Bartók's new orchestral work, Music for Strings, Percussion and Celesta, was given its first performance by the Basle Philharmonic Orchestra under its conductor, Paul Sacher. The first movement is one of the great fugues of this century; its subject was quoted in Fig. 20. The motivic concentration is as striking as Webern's. There is no counter-subject since the fugue is treated monothematically – that is, the subject serves as its own counter-subject. The tonal centre is A, which the chromatic fugue

Fig. 74

subject grows out from and returns to in unison at the end of the movement. The entries are a fifth apart (both upwards and downwards) and the climax is reached when E♮ and E♭ are played *fff* (bar 56). Here there are two points to make. First, the dynamics of this movement are based on a graded crescendo, from *pp* through *p*, *mp*, *f* and *ff* to *fff* (climax), and then back to *pp* and *ppp*. The second concerns the two clashing notes heard at the

Fig. 75a ∧   Fig. 75b ∨

Fig. 75c ∧ **Fig. 75d** ∨

climax, E♮ and E♭: the former is the tonal dominant of A, the latter a diminished fifth an equal distance from both the A above and the A below. This is what is known as the 'geographical' halfway. Canonic entries have already been introduced in the first part of the fugue (see Fig. 75a), but after the climax the subject returns, now in inverted canonic style (see Fig. 75b). The subject is also simultaneously played in both its original and inverted forms (see Figs 75c and 75d).

The reader is advised to listen to Bartók's 'barbaric' fugue in *The Miraculous Mandarin* and the finale of his Concerto for Orchestra for further illuminating examples.

Stravinsky too paid homage to Bach, as can be observed in the second movement of his Symphony of Psalms. His subject is an ingenious neo-baroque theme directly influenced by Bach's *Musical Offering*. Compare the opening bars of Bach's subject (Fig. 76) – or, to be more precise, Frederick the Great's (as it was he who suggested it to Bach) – with Stravinsky's (Fig. 77). Obviously

Fig. 76 ∧ **Fig. 77** ∨

Stravinsky's corresponding bars have a twist to them, as there is a leap from e♭'' up an augmented fifth to b♮'', the leading note of C minor. In bar 2 there is a diminished repetition of the opening four notes, which urges the pace on a little. The answer is

Fig. 78

orthodox, being on the dominant, and the counter-subject follows baroque procedures, with inversion and all (see Fig. 78).

But there is more: Stravinsky gives the four-part mixed choir a new subject, which he then combines with the first one, thus writing what is called a double fugue. In order to illustrate clearly what is happening Fig. 79 gives only the combination of the two subjects, and the other parts are left out. Double fugue, inversion, diminution and the like are technical means that enable the composer to express his musical ideas in an elaborate manner, as Stravinsky's Symphony of Psalms shows.

Fig. 79

Hindemith was not only a leading figure among the neoclassicists, but also influential as an educator through his music and his writings on music. In this he followed in the steps of Bach, who wrote inspired, but nevertheless didactic, compositions, such as two-part inventions and three-part sinfonias. In his *Ludus tonalis* Hindemith set out to give students 'Studies in Counterpoint,

Tonal Organization and Piano Playing'. Its Praeludium (see Fig. 80a) is followed by twelve fugues, interspersed with eleven Interludiums, and then a Postludium (see Fig. 80b), which is the Praeludium played backwards.

Fig. 80a ∧ **Fig. 80b** ∨

The sixth fugue, for three voices in E♭ major, demonstrates Hindemith's chromatic thinking as well as his adherence to tonality (see Fig. 81a). It ends on an enharmonic spelling of a second inversion of the tonic triad of E♭ major (see Fig. 81b), which

Fig. 81a ∧ **Fig. 81b** ∨

directly leads to the Interludium following it in the same key. In the eleventh fugue (in B major; see Fig. 82) Hindemith telescopes the fugal idea and the canonic form. This is not unlike Webern, albeit in an entirely different, tonally oriented style, based on his theory of an acoustically calculated tonal relationship.

Fig. 82

Finally, we now turn to Shostakovich. The influences on his musical personality are manifold, but it is possible to pinpoint three masters who left a marked impact on his thinking: Bach, Beethoven and Mahler. It was at the beginning of the 1950s that he composed the Twenty-four Preludes and Fugues for piano, which are something of a twentieth-century answer to Bach's '48'. There is, indeed, a deliberate similarity between them. Compare, for example, the first Prelude in C major, Bk 1, of Bach (Fig. 83a) and the first Prelude, also in C major, of Shostakovich (Fig. 83b).

Fig. 83a ∧ **Fig. 83b** ∨

Both Hindemith and Shostakovich arranged their fugues in a different systematic order from that of Bach. Shostakovich alternated major and minor keys in an ascending order of fifths (C major, A minor, G major, E minor and so on), an idea which may have been borrowed from Chopin's Preludes.

It is quite apparent from the above illustrations that polyphonic thinking, as inherited from the Middle Ages, Renaissance and eighteenth century, had a major role to play in the evolution of twentieth-century music. In their compositions, whether they are of tonal or serial orientation, several now renowned modern masters have relied heavily on motivic unity and intelligibility. In general, one could stipulate that the more complex the chromatic organization of a composition, the greater the composer's reliance on contrapuntal thematic unity. Webern's serial music is a case in point.

In the next chapter we turn to examining the notation of new sounds.

CHAPTER TWO

Notating New Sounds: *some aspects of modern musical notation — pitch, volume, silence and noise, dynamics, duration, rhythm*

Notation, the working-out of compositions, is primarily an ingenious expedient for catching an inspiration, with the purpose of exploiting it later. But notation is to improvisation as the portrait to the living model. It is for the interpreter to resolve the rigidity of the signs into the primitive emotion.

FERRUCCIO BUSONI

General considerations

In Western musical tradition from the late sixteenth century to the beginning of the twentieth musical notation remained largely unchanged. The system of using five staves with an elaborate series of symbols to indicate both the horizontal (that is, melody, time, rhythm) and the vertical (harmony, instrumentation) aspects of music was by and large felt to be adequate for even the most complicated musical statements during this long time. Thus, for example, a fugue by Bach (see Fig. 84, from the '48' Bk 1 No. XXIV) or an orchestral passage from Wagner's *Tristan und Isolde* (see Fig. 85) found satisfactory written expression within this system. Even in scores in this century the traditional system was and still is in good use, as is the case in Bartók's Concerto for Orchestra of 1943 (see Fig. 86).

Nevertheless, it is safe to say that the old system of notating music has been expanded or drastically altered, and in many cases

Fig. 84

Fig. 85

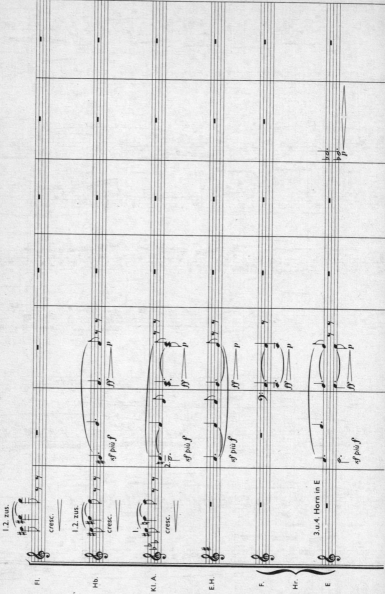

Fig. 86

abandoned altogether and replaced by other, often highly idiosyncratic notations and explanatory notes given by modern composers. Nowadays the problems facing a performer are not only
learning and interpreting a piece of music, difficult enough with a
familiar notational system, but also learning and deciphering an
entirely new style of notation beforehand. Earle Brown's score for
December 1952 (see Fig. 87) is an elegant example of idiosyncratic
musical graphics, reminiscent of one of Mondrian's paintings
rather than musical notation indicating pitch, duration and
dynamics.

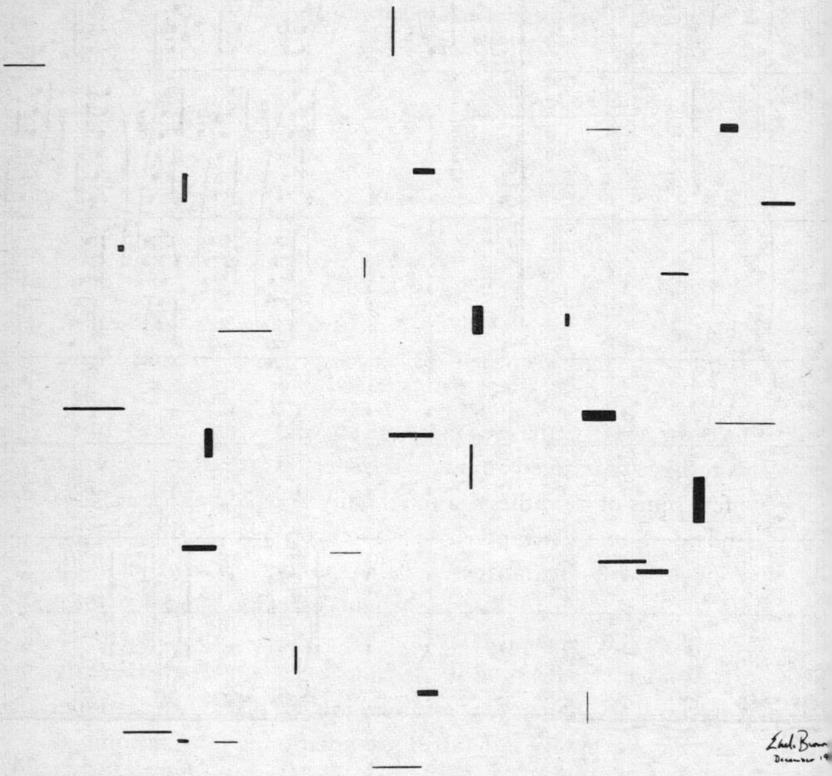

Fig. 87

Whatever modifications have taken place in musical notation – and there have been many, including the increased use of verbal indications since the nineteenth century – from the later part of the sixteenth century they were all related to a unifying system. The example in Fig. 87, however, illustrates a tendency among some twentieth-century composers to defy and abandon the familiar notational system in favour of a highly individual set of signs which need explanation. Some composers have confronted us with the privatization of musical notation with little or no reference whatsoever to the traditional central system. Imagine a writer who prefers to express the statement 'The sun was shining for a long time' by a private set of signs, such as:

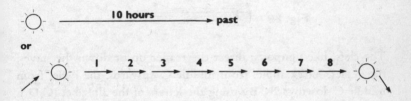

Possible, but it calls for explanation between writer and reader. So, with some musical notation, composers must explain themselves to performers.

Since the end of the Second World War a notational babel seems to have developed among composers. To this day there are very few signs of a synthesis, a universally accepted agreement on a standard. Some attempts have, however, been made in this direction, notably by Jacques Chailley in *Les notations musicales nouvelles* (1950), Erhard Karkoschka in *Das Schriftbild der neuen Musik* (1966) and Howard Risatti in *New Music Vocabulary* (1975). But composers by and large do not seem to be particularly perturbed by the apparent proliferation of various notational systems. Indeed, highly individualistic notation is seen by some as an integral part of the composition, giving it not only a characteristic stamp but also protection from philistine hostility, as is the case with Cornelius Cardew, who wrote: 'Pieces need camouflage to protect them from hostile forces in the early days of their life. One kind of protection is provided by the novelty and uniqueness of notation; few musicians will take the trouble to decipher and learn the notations unless they have a positive interest in performing the works.'

Before looking in more detail at some of the alternative notations, we might do well to remind ourselves about some basics of the traditional Western system. In traditional musical notation staves, clefs and notes are needed to indicate pitch (see Fig. 88).

Fig. 88

The clefs, like signposts, direct the reader up or down the staves, the G clef, for example, from middle C upwards, the F clef from middle C downwards. By using the letters of the alphabet (C D E F G A B) for the notes, combined with the understanding of the positions of middle C, the G clef and bass clef, it does not take long to work out the position of various pitches. To a large extent a system of musical notation reflects the style of the music it attempts to preserve in writing. Our musical notation, which uses seven letters of the alphabet within the octave, is diatonic and tonally conceived, with an emphasis on melody and tonal harmony. Much new music, though, is not tonal, and melody, in the traditional sense, no longer represents a dominating consideration. Several composers of this century felt that as their intentions and styles were different from the traditional ones, their method of notation had to reflect this change. A number of ingenious attempts have been made to classify the resulting proliferation of notational methods under various headings. Whether these classifications will survive the test of time and become absorbed into our musical jargon remains to be seen. Here, for reasons of simplicity, three plausible categories are offered:

new sounds in old notation; new notations mixed with old; the abandonment of traditional notation.

New sounds in old notation

The fragment from Anton Webern's *Klavierstück* Op. post. in Fig. 89 illustrates how the old notation can work in rendering on paper an entirely new compositional style. The tempo indication refers to the minuet; clefs and time signature are clearly indicated. There are two treble clefs in bar 1, treble and bass clefs in bars 2 and 3, a temporary return to two treble clefs and then back to treble and bass clefs again and so on. This gives further emphasis to the intervallic jumpiness of the melodic contour, which is characterized by, among other things, the predominant use of sevenths (for example bb–a♮'). Note the constant changing of accidentals, as well as the dense fluctuation of dynamic marks. Seemingly all is well. There are problems, however, which need to be considered. Our musical notation is founded on tonal notation (see the explanations of tonality and atonality in Chapter One and Chapter Three), with constant references to pitch centre and triadic thinking. This harmonic implication is reflected in our notation. Webern's piano composition is atonal and his accidentals have no tonal implication as they do not 'lead' to or 'gravitate' towards a key (central pitch) in the traditional sense. The unaccustomed reader and pianist is therefore likely to be bewildered by the maze of signs which do not lead the hands in familiar directions. On the contrary, it avoids them. During this century accidentals have by and large been used quite flexibly by many composers. It is interesting to note that in 1923 Arnold Schoenberg was already contemplating the problem when he wrote:

The notes c d e f g a b would in general always be given the natural sign, without pedantic exaggeration, i.e. when it is clear in some other way, then the simpler alternative is followed, for in modern music it is difficult

Im Tempo eines Menuetts

Fig. 89

to keep in one's mind throughout a long bar, whether some note has already occurred with a sharp or a flat. This rule is only at all sensible and justified in music where, the modulation rate being slow, a melody is nearly always built on one of the familiar scales.

Then he goes on:

However after they occur, the notes c-sharp, d-flat, d-sharp, e-flat, e-sharp, etc. are (again without pedantry) provided with sharp or flat; this usually applies even when they occur a second time in the bar, unless things are made absolutely clear in some way.

This is followed by a brisk criticism of the notational procedure of Béla Bartók and Ernst Krenek, who, he believed, were not

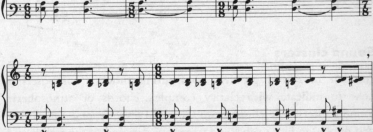

Fig. 90

consistent and logical in their notations. Neither Bartók nor Krenek needs defending. The logic of some of Bartók's musical spelling is based on employing the traditional directional rules of sharps and flats whereby sharps and naturals move upwards and flats downwards, as in the example from Bartók's 'Free Variations' (*Mikrokosmos* Vol. VI No. 140) in Fig. 90. The spelling of the accidentals in the bass gives emphasis to the melodic curve (see Fig. 91), as does the top line (see Fig. 92). Since on the piano E♭ and D♯ are enharmonically the same, it would be possible to spell Fig. 90 as in Fig. 93, but Bartók's version is better for melodic reasons.

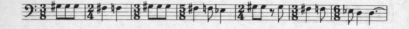

Fig. 91 ∧   **Fig. 92** >

Fig. 93

Sound clusters

Another notational problem confronting modern composers is how to indicate with clarity complex chords or atmospheric sound clusters. The chord from Charles Ives's *Concord Sonata* that was quoted in Fig. 54 makes a strenuous demand of the reader and player because there is not enough space to indicate the sharps where they should be, next to the notes they modify. It was Ives and Henry Cowell who in the first decades of this century started to practise what are called cluster chords, that is, the simultaneous sounding of a large number of seconds. Cowell's ingenious solution was to link them together with the traditional stems of duration between the required lower and upper notes, as in *The Hero Sun* for piano (see Fig. 94). The way to perform the 'noise' elements

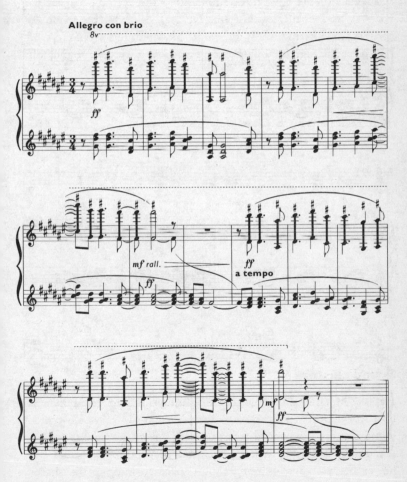

Fig. 94

here is to use the right forearm on the black keys. In order to indicate this the sharp sign is written over the cluster; the natural sign would indicate white keys.

In his 'Night's Music' for piano Bartók spells the cluster by

Fig. 95

separating the flattened notes from the sharpened ones for better visual grasp and adds that the cluster should be executed with the left hand (see Fig. 95).

These examples illustrate a modern tendency to divest individual notes of some of their weight and of the importance of their accuracy and to emphasize instead atmospheric effects (colour), rhythm and dynamics.

Noise

At this point we turn to the vexed problem of noise. We know that sound is produced by vibration; without vibration there is no sound. If the vibration is regular, the resulting sound will have a definite pitch (for example middle C = 256 vps). This is referred to as a musical sound. If the frequency is irregular, the resulting sound is labelled noise. That is the scientific and traditional view concerning sound. During the twentieth century we have witnessed the emancipation of noise to such an extent that, in terms of aesthetics, it would now be rather misleading to carry on stressing the traditional divisions between music and noise. Modern composers use any sound material or any form they find fit in order to express themselves in their compositions. Igor Stravinsky's *Rite of Spring* offers sound effects, written in conventional notation, in which melody and harmony are secondary to the overwhelmingly percussive rhythmic emphasis. There are moments when the musical pitch, whether seen from its horizontal or vertical aspects, is entirely subordinated to the stylized harsh brutality of the rhythmic accentuation (see Fig. 49).

Erik Satie's *Vexations* for piano, on the other hand, is a contemplative piece of music without bar-lines, phrasing or dynamic marks (see Fig. 96). The tempo indication is 'Très lent'. The composer, who was never reticent about making fanciful and often cryptic comments of his music, said: 'In order to play this motif for oneself 840 times in succession, one had best prepare oneself in the deepest silence by serious immobilities.'

Fig. 96

Notating silence

The signs for notating duration are closely linked to pitch notation. The principle is based on geometrical progression:

$$\mathbf{o} \;=\; \mathbf{\textstyle\bigcup\bigcup} \;=\; \mathbf{\textstyle\bigcup\bigcup\bigcup\bigcup} \;=\; \text{♫ ♫ ♫ ♫} \;=\; \text{etc.}$$

Fig. 97

The signs for the corresponding representation of silence are:

$$\rule{1em}{0.3em} \;=\; \mathbf{o} \quad \rule{1em}{0.3em} \;=\; \mathbf{\textstyle\bigcup} \quad \text{₹} \;=\; \mathbf{\textstyle\bigcup} \quad \text{૪} \;=\; \mathbf{\textstyle\bigcup} \; \text{etc.}$$

Fig. 98   **Fig. 99 >**

As might be expected, a traditional instrumental score shows signs of pitch, duration, rests and so on, as in Fig. 99, from Prokofiev's Classical Symphony. The indication of many empty bars for those instruments which are not playing at a given time was felt by some composers to be superfluous. Accordingly, they decided to leave out unnecessary rest signs and silent empty bars altogether. This resulted in a visually fragmented style of scoring. Imagine Prokofiev's score in Fig. 99 without the unnecessary rest symbols and with the empty bars left out for good measure.

Silence

It should be noted that silence, which has always had great practical purpose (such as giving breathing space to the poor musician) and artistic significance (for example in creating dramatic effect), has grown increasingly important during this century. Expressionistic intensity is much enhanced by the effective use of silence, as can be seen in Schoenberg's Six Little Piano Pieces Op. 19 No. 2 (Fig. 100), where the 'pitch events' (ten in number) are embedded in silence marked by rest indications. The

Fig. 100

opening bar of Webern's Six Bagatelles for string quartet Op. 9 No. 1 consists of three notes and eight rests (see Fig. 101).

The partial or total absence of sound is indeed a legitimate element of music, and gives the listener not only a sense of expectation and suspense, but also time for retrospection. Many examples of it can be found in the repertory of such modern composers as Boulez, Cage and Ligeti. The most notorious instance

Fig. 101 >

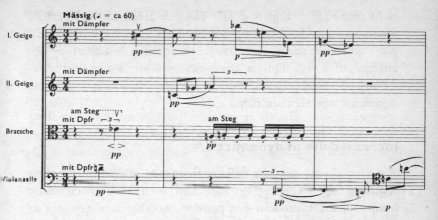

is, of course, John Cage's *4' 33"*. The title refers to the length of silence requested by the composer, during which one may contemplate whatever sounds are heard, be it one's heartbeat or the buzzing of a fly. This is obviously not art music, but Zen-influenced contemplation. Both noise and silence have become significant aspects of our culture.

Increased use of dynamics

We have already seen the striking frequency of dynamic changes requested by Webern (Fig. 89). This is another characteristic feature of much modern composition, notably in the works of Boulez and Stockhausen. In some instances this sensibility to dynamic nuances can reach a point where virtually every note has a specific dynamic mark, as in Stockhausen's *Kreuzspiel* (see Fig.

Fig. 102 ∧   **Fig. 103** ∨

102). It is possible, however, to go too far with unrealistic requests. Boulez's *Structures I* (see Fig. 103) seems to call for electronic equipment, as no pianist can possibly produce what is marked: the crescendo in the second bar is unplayable.

Rhythm

The combination of duration and rhythm enables composers to express time. In many ways the 'art of sound' is also the 'art of time'. That is why S. K. Langer, in her remarkable book *Feeling and Form: A Theory of Art*, wrote: 'What, then, is the essence of all music? The creation of virtual time, and its complete determination by the movement of audible forms.'

In traditional music we have grown accustomed to hearing and feeling rhythms which are systematized into groups of regular pulsations of two, three and four (called simple times) and their compound combinations, six, nine and twelve (called compound times). These metrical units are grouped into characteristic bars, examples of which are given in Fig. 104. The bar-lines thus serve to hold together and make comprehensible the whereabouts of the

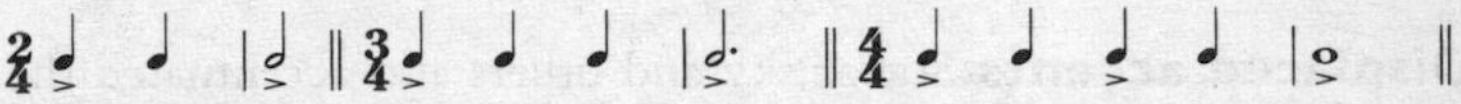

Fig. 104a ∧ **Fig. 104b** ∨

main beats, but the 'tyranny of bar-lines' was resented by many composers who were seeking a freer rhythmic flow. That is why Ligeti, in his notes concerning the performance of his composition *Lontano*, went out of his way in stressing that 'bar-lines serve only as a means of synchronization; bar-lines and beats never mean an accentuation, the music must flow smoothly'.

Debussy also looked for flexibility of rhythm, as can be seen in his two books of *Préludes*. In 'Danseuses de Delphes', for instance, the time signatures are 3/4 and 4/4; in 'Feux d'artifice' the time signatures are 4/8, 2/8, 4/8, 3/8 and 5/8. The third movement of Ravel's Sonatine for piano contains the following changes of time signature: 3/4, 5/4, 4/4 and 2/4. The list could easily be multiplied. The greatest rhythmic surprise is likely to be associated with the name of Stravinsky. The audience at the first performance of his *Rite of Spring* in 1913 was shocked by, among other things, its rhythmic irregularity, which triggered uncertainty and convulsive agitation (see Fig. 105). The rhythmic excitement here is brought about by Stravinsky's swift change of time signature.

Fig. 105

Displaced accents Stravinsky and others also accentuated the rhythm on unexpected beats within the expected metre (see Fig. 106).

Fig. 106

Asymmetric rhythm Yet another characteristic of modern music is the use of asymmetric rhythmic patterns, such as five or seven beats within a bar. Their grouping is based on the combination of duple and triple time, for example: 3 + 2 = 5, or 2 + 3 = 5; 4 + 3 = 7, or 3 + 4 = 7, or 2 + 3 + 2 = 7; and so forth.

In each case the inner accent changes according to the combinations. These patterns are popular in central and eastern Europe and Asia and are commonly referred to as Bulgarian rhythm. Both Bartók and Stravinsky, to mention only two of the most prominent figures in twentieth-century music, were noted for using them; Fig. 107 is an extract from Bartók's 'Bulgarian Rhythm' (*Mikrokosmos* Vol. IV No. 115).

Fig. 107

Polyrhythm Polyrhythm or, as it is sometimes called, polymetric or cross rhythm, is generally the combination of two or more metric accents. It is popular in Africa and was prominent in Western music in the fourteenth century. After the Renaissance it largely disappears, though there are occasional examples to be found in the works of Bach and even Mozart, as the finale of Act I of his opera *Don Giovanni* illustrates (see Fig. 108). Several twentieth-century composers resurrected this method of rhythmic organization, making polyrhythm one of the permanent features of twentieth-century music. Names such as Bartók, Berg, Carter, Hindemith, Ives, Messiaen, Stockhausen and Stravinsky come instantly to mind. Fig. 109 quotes contemporary examples, Stravinsky's *Petrushka* and Berg's Lyric Suite.

Fig. 108

i. 109a

Fig. 109a contd.

Fig. 109b

Ostinato rhythm Ostinato rhythm is a device based on the obstinate repetition of a rhythmic pattern or figure (see Fig. 110, from Bartók's 'Ostinato', *Mikrokosmos* Vol. VI No. 146). Its

Fig. 110

presence in art music can be traced back to the thirteenth century. In the context of its twentieth-century revival, however, it should be seen not only as an anti-romantic, percussively direct procedure, but also as an amalgamation of African and Oriental musical influences with Western musical thinking.

Variable metres Further interesting rhythmic ideas were developed by Boris Blacher and Elliott Carter. Blacher, in his *Ornamente* for piano composed in 1950, introduced the concept of writing music based on rhythmic patterns called variable metres for the first time. In this technique the metre is systematically changed by increasing (or decreasing) the nomination of the time signatures, for example: 2/8, 3/8, 4/8, 5/8 and so on.

Metric modulation Carter, under the influence of Ives, evolved a more complex system, called metric modulation. The purpose of this rhythmic organization is to enable the composer to express rhythmic shifts of great nuance and polyrhythmic freedom, albeit in a highly ordered form, in both rhythmic pulsations and tempi. The basic concept is somewhat related to cross rhythm, or cross-metric thinking. Metric pulse and tempo are made to 'modulate' via a subtle shift from the old to the new as shown in Fig. 111. This is, of course, a simple example, but it suffices to illustrate

Fig. 111

the vast rhythmic and tempo-changing possibilities inherent in the idea. Some of Carter's scores, among them the String Quartet No. 2 (see Fig. 112), give a very complex rhythmic texture. In a

Fig. 112

book by Allen Edwards, *Flawed Words and Stubborn Sounds*, Carter, in connection with his preoccupation with finding a way to free himself from the limiting similarity of bar-lines structured by strong beats, said: 'The result in my own music was, first of all, the way of evolving rhythms and continuities now called "metric modulation", which I worked out in the composition of my Cello Sonata in 1948.'

Fractional rhythmic organization The idea of a fractional augmentation or diminution of a rhythmic pattern is a method which Olivier Messiaen evolved from his long association with Indian music. Its basic principle is to add or subtract not half-values, as in traditional music (see Fig. 97), but greater or lesser values of durations. We know, for example, that the sign o equals the length of four crotchets: o = ♩ ♩ ♩ ♩ . If one augments it by a fourth (one crotchet), the resulting pattern is o + ♩ = o ♩. Conversely, if diminution is required, o − ♩ = ♩. . If the rhythmic pattern in Fig. 113a is augmented

Fig. 113a ∧ **Fig. 113b** ∨

by a fourth, the result will be Fig. 113b. The potential of this thinking is vast and it opens up fascinating possibilities. No wonder that such avant-garde composers as Boulez and Stockhausen found these ideas so challenging. As Boulez put it:

The notational use of the opposition between multiplication and division of the unit will, moreover, give rise to striking contrasts due to the broader span of values brought into play . . . Interaction of these various methods of organization can be extremely fertile, and will create an inexhaustible variety of objects – in the same way as in the field of pitch.

Non-retrogradable rhythm Messiaen's other idea concerning the organization of rhythm was what is rather clumsily referred to as non-retrogradable rhythm. This is based on symmetrically grouped rhythmic patterns, such as ♩ ♪♩ ♪♩. The main reason for retrograde technique is to create variety and continuation. Non-retrograde rhythmic structuring, by having two symmetrical wings, makes retrograde differentiation impossible, thus giving the music a rhythmic sameness.

New notations mixed with old

However unconventional the musical problems discussed so far, they were expressed in traditional musical notation, a notation which, as we have seen, is still largely in use. We now turn briefly to another development of musical notation, whereby a composer combines the old system with his or her personal method. To start

Fig. 114   Fig. 115

with a simple example, Fig. 114 means g′. In his *Transición II* Mauricio Kagel, by adding an arrow (see Fig. 115), indicates that what has to be played is any note above the given g′. A downward arrow, of course, indicates that a performer should play any note below a given note. What is asked for is not a specific note, but a specific range (that is, any high note, middle note or low note), to be played in a quasi-improvisatory manner.

Fig. 116 ©1963 by C. F. Peters Corporation, New York. Reproduced by permission of Peters Edition Ltd, London

The performer as composer

A fascinating example of a work in which the composer invites
the performer to take part in the creative process of composition is
the first movement of Morton Feldman's *Last Pieces* for piano (see
Fig. 116). At first glance the notation is conventional, though it
quickly becomes apparent that, as in Satie's *Vexations* (see Fig. 96),
bar-lines, phrasing, dynamic marks (except a general reference,
'soft') and the duration of notes are all left to the performer's
discretion. Rest assured this is not laziness on the part of the
composer, but evidence of a different attitude to compositional
procedures. Many composers see the relationship between composer and performer at a heightened level of shared creative
responsibility.

At the other extreme we find the scientific precision with
which Stockhausen notated his *Klavierstück X* (see Fig. 117). It was

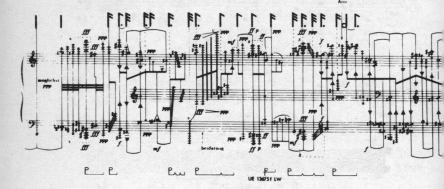

Fig. 117

based on the application of the old system, into which a series of
new signs was amalgamated, such as:

accelerando: ritenuto: very fast:

Penderecki, in his *Threnody for the Victims of Hiroshima* (see Fig. 118), replaced the old time signature, tempo marks and so on with his own precise indication of timing in seconds, and represented the required sound effects and dynamics by a black line of varying dimensions moving up and down.

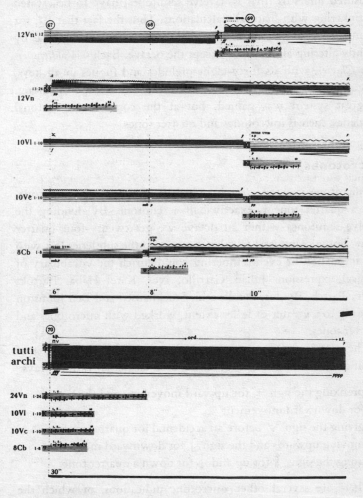

Fig. 118

Unjust to just intonation

Our tonal system stems from an elegant and logical system which is nevertheless based on an acoustic cheat. In order to divide up the octave as we now know it, it was found that twelve equally measured intervals (that is, twelve semitones) have to be created by tinkering with 'natural' calculations. Thus the fact that B♯, for example, works out higher in pitch than C♮ was overcome by slightly altering all intervals except the octave. Bach's *Wohltemperirtes Clavier*, with its forty-eight preludes and fugues in all keys, was among the first artistic vindications of this method of tuning. A great system was gained, but at the cost of certain tonal subtleties, such as microtones and quarter tones.

Microtones

A microtone is a tone (pitch) which is smaller than a semitone, and a quarter tone is exactly half a semitone. By dividing the twelve semitones within an octave we get twenty-four quarter tones. Some composers felt that a return to the subtleties lost with just intonation or even tempering could enrich the vocabulary of musical expression. Julián Carrillo, Ives, Karel Hába, Bartók, Harry Partch, Boulez, Penderecki, Stockhausen and Ben Johnston have all, to a greater or lesser extent, worked with microtones and quarter tones.

The notation of microtones is not easy. Within the context of traditional notation, the problem has been tackled in various ways:

(a) prefixing the sign + for upward movement and the sign − for downward movement
(b) giving the sign ∨ before an accidental for quarter tones moving upwards and the sign] for downward movement
(c) using the signs ↑ for up and ↓ for down a quarter tone

There are several other microtone indications, of which the most ingenious is Carrillo's numerical representation of the frac-tions of each of the notes. Apart from the indications of duration, tempo and dynamics, all other traditional elements of notation, including the staves, have been replaced (see Fig. 119, from his *Preludio a Cristobal Colón*).

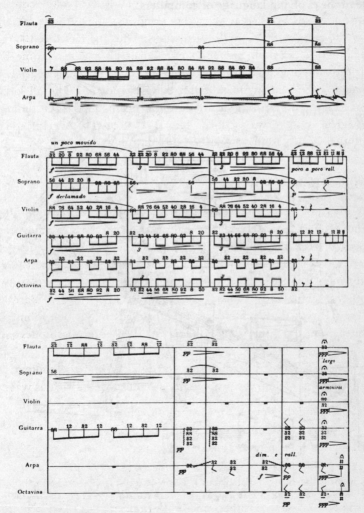

Fig. 119

It is fair to say that our traditional system has now been stretched to its limit and that we are in need of some notational development which will enable composers, yet again, to notate their music by means of a universal system. The answer is likely to lie in the evolving language of computers.

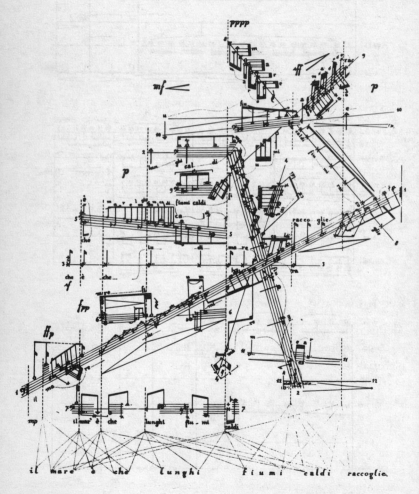

Fig. 120

The abandonment of traditional notation

Attempts to replace traditional notation with diagrams, graphic descriptions or numerical and verbal references have mushroomed since the 1950s.

Graphic score

Looking at the splendid graphic score of Brown (Fig. 87), we are confronted with a notational reference which allows the player (or players) to do whatever he or she wants. The horizontal and vertical lines, as well as their proportions, can be interpreted as pitches, durations or dynamics. Moreover, further possibilities can be found by turning the score clockwise or anticlockwise. Sylvano Bussotti's *Siciliano* is a pleasure to the eyes while being a quite accurate representation of the composer's intentions (see Fig. 120). The sign ⊢ means up a quarter tone, ⧺ up three quarter tones and ⌐ colourless; upward and downward slanting staves refer to faster and slower tempi. Behind the pictorial image there is a musical message.

Eye music and word-painting

At this point it is worth reminding ourselves that there is nothing new in composers fancifully playing around in symbolic and pictorial ways, for this has occurred since the Middle Ages. The heart-shaped anthology in Fig. 121a dates from the fifteenth century; in Fig. 121b, from Byrd's 'Come, woeful Orpheus' (a madrigal), the words 'sharps' and 'flats' are notated accordingly; in Fig. 121c, from Bach's *St Matthew Passion*, the word 'crucify' is symbolically syncopated ♪♩ ♪, giving a visual interpretation of the cross. Furthermore, it was customary among fifteenth- and sixteenth-century composers to use blackened notes for such words as 'dark' and 'night'. An outstanding example is Josquin des Prés's

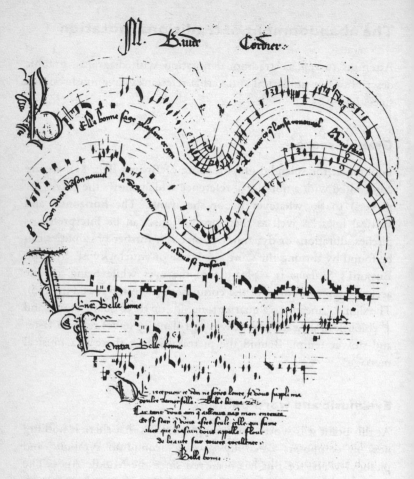

Fig. 121a ∧ **Fig. 121b** ∨

of sour - est sharps and un -

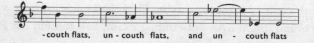

-couth flats, un - couth flats, and un - couth flats

Fig. 121c

'Lament on the death of Johan. Ockeghem', which he composed entirely in black notes in order to express grief and sorrow visually as well as musically.

Kagel's pattern

In an article entitled 'Translation-Rotation', which Kagel wrote for *Die Reihe* in 1960, he introduced a compositional formula which is based on the inventive use of a geometric pattern. By rotating this pattern at a fixed point around an axis, it is possible to create sound patterns:

Rising or falling as directions in a series of notes are components of a geometry in two dimensions; connecting lines between the combined directions of several notes create surfaces that can be articulated temporally

and dynamically. For example, this 'figure' can be extended;

a delay on the B could have the following effect  and if

dynamics are added, a dimension is gained which causes a spatial accentu-

ation in the figure:

If we investigate the figure divorced from the musical stave   the

earlier distance between the notes is no longer an expression of a temporal sequence; the perimeter, accentuated by four dots, is free of any
temporal function and therefore cannot force any directional movement
on our attention.

The isolation of the figure from its complementary relationship to a
musical process serves for an experiment. There is now no temporal
sequence from left to right to fix the orientation of the figure, so
movement becomes possible if one refers the figure to a musical parameter
(for example, pitch).

The following is the result of the application of two simple *categories of
movement*:

I. *Translation* as a simple, straight-line shift of two (or more) similar (or
dissimilar) forms along one or more constant or variable axes:

Example 1

Thus the manipulation of a visual form (or forms) on the staff
enables a composer to 'design' music and either to notate it as a
symbolic, geometric form or to translate it into musical notation.

We list the following *coupled categories*:

Screwing, as a coupling of straight-line and circular shifts around a
screwing point and a constant axis of translation.

Rotation develops really as a changed principle of screwing – when one represents time as a (straight-line) sliding axis. If one hears successively the basic shape and a shape derived from it, this has the effect, temporally, of a turning in a certain direction.

Rotation and mirroring as a turning of the basic shape around one turning point and one mirror-axis.

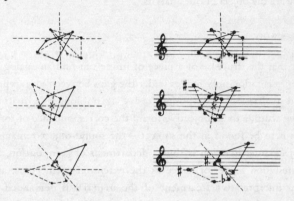

The difference between this and the usual sort of rotation is that here the derived shape turns on top of the basic shape.

Rotation and spreading as a circular and centripetal shift (with regular or irregular growth of the basic shape) around a *spiral* axis.

Other coupled categories of movement could be: mirroring and spreading, translation and jamming, screwing and spreading, etc. All these categories of movement can be interpreted from the most various points of view. An investigation of all the combinatorial possibilities of these categories can only be justified by the intention to include them in a composition. In the main text of this article we have tried to dispense with a comprehensive and systematic treatment since, in view of the multiplicity of the resulting connections, there is no room for such a development within the framework of this treatise. Our experience is based mainly on translative and rotative forms of shift (in the electronic piece 'Transición I' and its instrumental pendant 'Transición II'); these therefore are the object of our analysis.

Kagel goes on:

The fact that the structure of a piece of music can find an analogy in the visual representation only makes wider the gaps between idea, representation and realization. Composing today is no longer a matter of a subjective attitude to an objective form; the correspondence of forms and methods is to be found in the subject – the sound-object remains as the only object. Interpretation is thus a department of composition, both in its manifestation in performance as the extension of the idea, and also when an interpretative treatment of the material is demanded by the perspectives of infinite possible points of combination in the internal articulation of the form.

Verbal score

Among other notational innovations, Kagel also employs verbal score. His verbal score (to be read from left to right) indicates duration (in seconds), dynamics and a verbal script. These instructions are given a joint reading by the players and then performed.

Cardew, who was one of the founding members of the Scratch Orchestra in London in 1969 and, for a while, believed that Scratch Music 'is the basis of the world, going on everywhere all the time', offered 1,001 activities for the performance of his scratch music. But in the hurly-burly of anarchistic verbal wit the music was somewhat lost, as the following selection of 'activities' will illustrate:

718 Swing a cat

719 Swing a Blue Whale

720 Up, up and away

721 Help an old lady across the road against her will

722 Drink a yard of ale

723 Drink a yard of whisky

724 Hold a special service in the memory of anyone attempting '723'

In a light-hearted spirit one is tempted to add to these activities 'Play the unplayable'.

Electronic music and notation

In general parlance the term 'electronic music' covers the range of all music which is electronically arrived at. It would be more correct, however, to apply it only in connection with those cases where tape, synthesizer and the computer are used. By confining the term to the operation of this equipment for the purpose of composing, we reach a less broad and more accurate description of electronic music. A fascinating aspect of electronic music is that its final form is recorded on magnetic tape, from which it can be directly performed. A score preserving the composer's intention is therefore not of primary importance. Nevertheless, some composers prepare scores, largely to enable them to synchronize electronically made music with live performance or to help the performer-technician play directly with electronic equipment guided by the composer's specific instructions.

A most attractive example of an electronic music score is Stockhausen's *Studie II* (see Fig. 122). Starting from the bottom, he indicates dynamics and then, using numbers, duration (in this case with reference to the speed at which the tape is played, 76.2 cmps). The various blocks at the top indicate pitch.

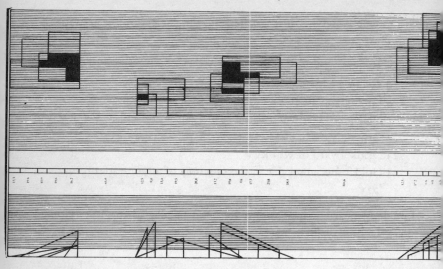

Fig. 122

This is, of course, a far cry from the conventional score. But it is an elegant technological instruction to be given to a technician, or technologically inclined musician, for realization. One could argue that with electronic music we have reached a point where the preservation of music is no longer a question of writing it down by using whatever system one may find appropriate. Electronic music does not need to be notated; it can be preserved by electronic means and, as long as there is electricity, performed at any time and anywhere by anyone. When it comes to electronic music, even the concert hall tradition is called into question.

In this chapter we have touched upon notational difficulties facing musicians, together with some of the changes in the ways music is recorded on paper which have taken place during this century. Having discussed some fundamental theoretical problems concerning modern music, we now turn to the vexed issue of forms.

CHAPTER THREE

Forms and Patterns: *motif, phrase, sentence, binary and ternary forms, rondo, theme and variations, passacaglia, suite, sonata form, symphony, concerto, concerto grosso, concerto for orchestra, chamber music, vocal styles, speech-melody, choral works, opera*

In music there is no form without logic, there is no logic without unity.

ARNOLD SCHOENBERG

In Chapter One we saw that such contrapuntal textures as writing for two or more parts, free imitation, canon and fugue presented patterns of construction which helped us to comprehend the ways in which a polyphonic piece of music is likely to unfold. We saw how important motivic reference is in drawing both the horizontal and vertical aspects of music into a homogeneous unity. Pitch, intervals, melody, time values, rhythm and chords all contribute towards that unity. From the moment sound is manipulated for artistic purposes every aspect of it is part of the musical form, its ordered manifestation. Even with compositions in which the ordered complexity of music is partly or totally negated, as is the case with some of the aleatory works of Cage for instance, the listener's reaction is disproportionately biased towards what has been omitted rather than what is actually being offered in the composition, as if in search of comprehensible clues.

Although it is true that every composition has its own characteristic structure, it is nevertheless possible to discriminate and categorize musical forms displaying various organizing principles that govern the overall relationship of their parts. This shows a continuum of classical or archetypal patterns which modern composers have absorbed and integrated into their styles. We have observed that one of the most important principles of compositional organization was the dichotomy of contrast and imitation/repetition. In a fugue, for example, the counter-subject contrasts with the subject; the answer is in tonal (harmonic) contrast to the subject (tonic subject and dominant answer); the episode contrasts with the exposition; the answer imitates the subject; the canon strictly imitates/repeats the leading voice; and so forth. Broadly speaking, the same principle can be applied to all formal organizations, since the often complex interplay of contrast and imitation/repetition is the foundation of most forms of music. The ternary form ABA, which is the form of the da capo aria, the usual form of the third movement of a classical symphony (minuet – trio – minuet or scherzo – trio – scherzo) and also that of most nocturnes, is based on both contrast and repetition.

We can now consider how some twentieth-century composers have structured their music. But before turning to larger units, let us remind ourselves of some of the smaller components of music: the motif, phrase and sentence.

The motif

A motif is the smallest intelligible unit of music. Normally, in order to be meaningful it has to consist of at least two notes and a well-defined rhythmic profile. As such, a motif is a coherent melodic unit which begs, as it were, for further development. The three-note motif (cell) on which the complete set of Webern's Concerto for nine instruments Op. 24 is based shows a composite structure of the utmost concentration (see Fig. 123).

Fig. 123a ∧   **Fig. 123b** ∨

*sound as written

The phrase

A phrase is made up of one or more motifs. In tonal music the end of a phrase is generally arrived at by a cadence. In music where tonality is weakened or altogether discarded, considerations other than cadences, such as rests, long notes, relative chordal relationships, serial units and natural breathing points, come into play. As phrasing refers to the division of a melody into its component parts, it is an open field for interpretation and misinterpretation. Bartók's careful phrasing is evident in the extract from his 'In the Style of a Folksong' (*Mikrokosmos* Vol. IV No. 100) in Fig. 124.

Fig. 124

The sentence

A sentence in music is not unlike a sentence in writing. It is a complete, meaningful statement with a full stop at the end. The common form of a musical sentence used to be symmetrical, for instance four bars plus four bars, giving a total length of eight bars. During the twentieth century, however, the 'tyranny of barlines' has been broken down and asymmetrical phrasing and sentencing are now the norm. Schoenberg's String Quartet No. 4 provides a fine example (see Fig. 125).

Fig. 125

'The principal function of form is to advance our understanding. By producing comprehensibility, form produces beauty' wrote Schoenberg. It is interesting to note that revolutionary as he was, Schoenberg's approach to forms of music was more or less a continuation of procedures of earlier periods, which he put to good use in the context of his atonal and serial compositions. As Nicholas Cook pointed out in his brilliant book *A Guide to*

In den ersten 4 Takten soll die rechte Hand durchaus *f*, die linke durchaus *pp* spielen

Fig. 126

Musical Analysis, the third of the Six Little Piano Pieces Op. 19 (see Fig. 126) 'doesn't sound like Brahms but it looks like Brahms. In other words the Brahmsian rhythm, phrasing, dynamics and texture are all there, it is just the notes that are wrong.' Of course, Cook's reference to wrong notes is not a value judgement of Schoenberg's piano piece, but a witty observation on Schoenberg's entirely new musical thinking, which is put across in a context where everything else is traditional. The work is freely atonal, and belongs to the expressionist period just before the First World War. It consists of nine bars in all, broken into the following phrases: three times two bars, one bar and two bars. Apart from the last, the phrases are characterized by a downward move of minor or major seconds. The piece is to be played very slowly. The dynamic marks for the first four bars call for a juxtaposition of *f* for the right hand and *pp* for the left; thereafter a gradual quietening down follows from *p* to *ppp*. The piece defies conventional analysis, yet the motivic unity is an outstanding component of this short, but extremely complex and thought-provoking, composition (see Fig. 127).

Fig. 127

The motivic relationship, which is sustained throughout, demonstrates the cohesive logic of Schoenberg's musical thinking. It is this interaction which gives his music, however bizarre it may seem at first hearing, a sense of unity; its real structure is neatly held together between the opening downward fifth and the closing upward fifth. One could even suggest that although tonality, in the traditional meaning of the word, is undermined and although there are so many chromatic twists and dissonances, this piece is at least *on* G. The last chord could be interpreted as a tonic ninth.

This general sketch highlights the music's main features, which can be recognized by repeated hearing; we need not concern ourselves with musicological debate.

Binary form

The second movement of Webern's Variations for Piano Op. 27 presents two clearly indicated divisions with repeat signs for both sections, characteristic of the classical binary structure AB (see Fig. 128). Within the misleadingly simple binary form Webern introduced a most demanding strict canon in contrary motion. The subject of the canon appears in the right hand and is immediately imitated by the left hand at a distance of only one quaver. It should be remembered that in a canon in contrary motion the two voices mirror each other: that is, if Bb goes down to A (a semitone) in one voice, the other voice will mirror it by going up a semitone, in our case from G♯ to A (a semitone). Thus in the first six bars the following pitch organization occurs:

> Bb A♮ C♯ B♮ D♮ C♮ F♯ F♮ E♮ G♯ G♮ Eb
> G♯ A♮ F♮ G♮ E♮ F♯ C♮ C♯ D♮ Bb B♮ Eb
> (D♯ = Eb)

Webern alternates the order of voice entries at bars 5, 8, 17 and 18: what was played in the right hand is played in the left hand and vice versa. The result is a constantly oscillating intervallic movement punctuated by four chordal entries made up of the sixth, seventh and eighth pitch degrees of the series. There are a few places where the two canonic voices meet in unison on the note A (bars 1, 9, 13 and 19) and on the note D♯ or enharmonic

Sehr schnell (♩ = ca 160)

Fig. 128

E♭ (bars 6 and 21). It is interesting to note that whereas the repetitions of the As are emphasized, the repetitions of D♯/E♭ are somewhat subordinated by introducing them in the form of grace notes. Obviously the recurrent As have a strategically important role because the various pitches move towards and then depart from them in unison. It would be hasty to conclude, though, that it represents a tonic, as one should not mistake the contrapuntal passing encounters of two voices in a serial composition with tonality; a junction is not necessarily a station. The time signature is 2/4, but because of rhythmic displacement the feeling is more like 3/8.

A more easily accessible composition of this century is the Prelude from Ravel's noble homage, *Le Tombeau de Couperin*. There the reader will find the clear-cut tonal relationships of E minor, B minor and C major, as well as a splendid selection of seventh and ninth chords and a plagal cadence at the end. A further example is Cage's sixteen sonatas for prepared piano (Sonatas and Interludes), which are all in binary form (AABB).

Ternary form

Ternary form is one of the most popular musical structures because it represents a pattern in which contrast and repetition are united: ABA. The arch-like symmetry gives this form a balanced wholeness. It has been put to good use by many twentieth-century composers.

Let us start with a simple example, 'The Little Shepherd' from Debussy's *Children's Corner* (see Fig. 129). It begins with a four-bar solo introduction of vague tonality; in bars 5–11 theme A appears and firmly establishes the tonality of A major via a dominant–tonic cadence; in bars 12–18 the contrasting theme B follows, ending on the dominant key, E major. A link of two bars

Fig. 129 >

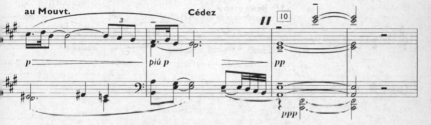

Fig. 129 contd.

(19–20) leads us back to the first theme, A, which is now extended by an inspired use of the little motif we first encountered at bar 6. The piece ends with the repetition of the cadential formula II⁷–V⁷–I.

The extension which appears at the return of theme A is a good example in miniature of the possible variation of the repeated theme in ternary form; it need not be exact. As Schoenberg put it, 'Never write what your copyist can compose for you.' The general structure of ternary form can also be varied in several ways: AABA, ABBA and ABAA, for example, are all in ternary form.

Bartók's contrapuntal thinking in the second movement of his Third Piano Concerto was referred to on pp. 56–7. Looking at the form of this movement, we find that it is based on the arch-like ternary principle, one of Bartók's most favoured forms. Bars 1–57 establish the thematic material of the A section; the B section runs from bar 58 to bar 88. At bar 89 the A section returns, but, as we have seen, the themes originally introduced by the piano are now played by the orchestra, and the piano brings in new contrapuntal material, all leading to the final reiteration of the opening motif (there are at least three motifs in section A) played by the string section of the orchestra and then on the piano (bars 134–7). In spite of all the thematic richness and contrapuntal intricacies, the overall musical form is based on the simple ternary structure ABA. In his search for structural logic and symmetry Bartók developed the ternary idea even further. In his Fourth String Quartet, for instance, perhaps under the influence of Berg, he extended the ternary form to the whole quartet by structuring its five movements in the following way: ABCBA. As each of the five movements is itself symmetrically structured, and the thematic relationship between the first and fifth movements and the second and fourth movements is close, one is confronted with an architectural design in sound and reminded of Goethe's description of architecture as 'frozen music'. An extended Bartókian arch form is also the structure underlying the third movement of his Music for Strings, Percussion and Celesta, where the pattern is ABCD<u>CB</u>A. The underlining of C and B indicates that in the repetition they are played simultaneously.

Finally we return again to Debussy, this time to his well-known

Prélude à l'après-midi d'un faune. This work has been analysed by many in numerous ways, with numerous conclusions. All display detailed reference to melodic and harmonic material, and make astute observations and illuminating points. What concerns us here, however, is not a bar-by-bar analysis of the whole composition, which is beyond the scope of this book, but the structural and aural perception of the music. Over several years I have asked my students to describe its general structure. Most thought that the overall shape was ABA, while some felt ABBA was perhaps more accurate. A few students heard subtle distinctions between thematic fragments that were barely As and also Bs, followed by a final return to A and a coda. What is revealing is that in each case the overall form was heard to be ternary. This was further substantiated by its harmonic plan, which, in spite of its ambiguous opening, also confirms a ternary form (see Fig. 130).

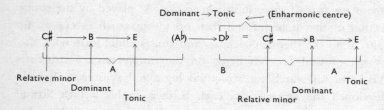

Fig. 130a ∧ **Fig. 130b** ∨

The reader is also advised to study Berg's music, and especially his Lyric Suite, which is a real treasure-house of compositional information. Its third movement, Allegro misterioso, is a scherzo in ternary form, ABA. Section A(i) is dodecaphonic; section B (Trio) is in free style; section A(ii) is a retrograde (mirror form) of section A(i).

The rondo

Contrast and unity (repetition) is the characteristic principle of ternary form. In the rondo form this is extended, in that ABA is further varied by new episode(s) and returns to the main theme: ABACA. In theory one could carry on going through the whole alphabet, but that would be too much of a good thing. Well-known examples from the orchestral repertory are Richard Strauss's *Till Eulenspiegel* and Milhaud's *Bœuf sur le toit*. For the sake of simplicity, here is the outline of an atmospheric piano piece from one of Bartók's *Ten Easy Pieces*, 'Evening in the Country': section A (bars 1–9) starts on E and ends on E minor tonic seventh; section B (bars 10–20) is based on a lively dance melody which ends over a C♯ minor chord; A returns (bars 21–9) with partly modified harmonic support; C is represented by a variation of B, which returns in an ornamented, melodically richly varied manner; A is played again, but now in a more extended way. Fig. 131 quotes the opening bars of each section. Obviously Bartók felt that B(ii), with its decorated melodic version of B(i), was sufficiently contrasting to equal episode C, giving the form AB(i)A-B(ii)A. Bartók's symmetrical thinking is displayed in miniature since each unit is independently in ternary form: ABA/BAB/ABA. Put together they form a rondo with interlocated material. The second movement of Berg's Lyric Suite, Andante amoroso, is in rondo form and based on the three themes in Fig. 132.

Some composers have an obsessive relationship with numbers, which on occasion can determine the structuring of their composi-

Fig. 131

Fig. 132a

Fig. 132b ∧ **Fig. 132c** ∨

tions. Berg was one such. The numbers 3, 5 and 23 had a particular significance for him; his opera *Wozzeck*, for example, is divided into 3 acts, each containing 5 scenes. The Lyric Suite is virtually dominated by the number 23: the first and fourth movements consist of 69 bars (3 × 23); the fifth movement is 460 bars long (20 × 23); the sixth movement is a fraction of the fifth, 46 (2 × 23); even a single movement can be subdivided by the number 23, as is the case with the third movement, where the division is 69 + 23 + 46 = 138 (6 × 23). Several composers, among them Debussy, Bartók and Stockhausen, found that certain numerical considerations helped them to form logical, well-proportioned structures. Two of the most striking and in a way related ideas used are the 'Fibonacci series' and the 'Golden section'.

The Fibonacci series is based on the findings of an adventurous medieval Italian mathematician called Leonardo Fibonacci, who introduced into Europe the decimal system and the use of zero, concepts he acquired from the Arabs. The main idea of the series is that each number is the sum of the preceding two numbers (0, 1, 1, 2, 3, 5, 8, 13, 21, 34 and so on). This method was applied by

Stockhausen in his *Klavierstück XI*. The Golden section has been used by architects from the time of the ancient Greeks. It is arrived at by dividing a distance into two parts in such a way that the ratio of the small section to the larger section is equal to the ratio of the larger section to the whole. Debussy's both small- and large-scale compositions (such as the well-known 'Cathédrale engloutie' for piano and *La Mer*) and Bartók's Music for Strings, Percussion and Celesta, among other works, were structured by using the Golden section. This is far from being the full picture, but it is sufficient to illustrate the extent to which numerical thinking can determine the length as well as the structure of a composition.

Theme and variations

The term 'theme and variations' refers to perhaps one of the oldest ways of making music in a more extended form: a theme is established and then elaborated on, bringing out the musical possibilities to be found in its melodic, rhythmic and harmonic profile. The principle of variations is based on repetition in which the contrasting elements are the variations themselves. The 'known', that is, the theme, remains more or less constant, while the 'unknown' is the way in which the theme is varied, usually by melodic, rhythmic, harmonic and colouristic modifications. The theme is normally clearly stated at the beginning of a set of variations and followed by a series of elaborations, the variations; there can be any number, though going beyond thirty-two is rare. The theme for variation is usually a melody written in binary or ternary form, but it can also be a musical sentence written either by the composer or borrowed from another composer's work, or taken from a folksong. A superb example of borrowing for this purpose is Britten's Variations and Fugue on a Theme of Purcell Op. 34 (also known as *The Young Person's Guide to the Orchestra*), the theme of which Britten took from Purcell's music for the play

Abdelazer. As Britten's intention is didactic, we hear the theme six times over before the variations proper begin: it is played *tutti,* by the woodwind, brass, strings, percussion and *tutti* again; this is followed by thirteen variations and finally a fugue, which is then combined with Purcell's theme in an apotheosis. The main theme is given in Fig. 133a and the first four bars of the fugue subject combined with the theme in Fig. 133b.

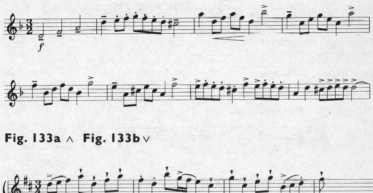

Fig. 133a ∧ **Fig. 133b** ∨

Now we turn to look more closely at Kodály's Variations on a Hungarian Folksong ('The Peacock'). It uses a popular theme with a politically charged text – the peacock symbolizes freedom and liberation from oppression. An introduction based on the penta-tonic theme (see Fig. 134a) leads to a solo statement of the theme on the oboe at bar 65 (see Fig. 134b). In order to give some idea of melodic, rhythmic and harmonic variations one fragment to illustrate each of these categories has been chosen:

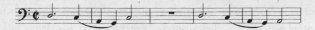

Fig. 134a ∧ **Fig. 134b** ∨

(a) melodic variation

Fig. 135 Variation VIII

(b) rhythmic variation

Fig. 136 Variation V

(c) harmonic variation

Fig. 137 Variation XI (B♭ minor)

From the pentatonic opening on d, Kodály leads through the sixteen variations to an energetic dance-like finale in which the coda (bars 632–710) triumphantly ends on an affirmative D major.

In connection with binary form (or division) we have already looked at the second movement of Webern's Variations for Piano. In the opening seven bars of the first movement the theme based on the twelve-note row (see Fig. 138a) is immediately varied in retrograde (see Fig. 138b); the left hand mirrors the right hand and at bar 4 their directions cross each other (see Fig. 138c). In fact, the theme itself appears at the outset in contrapuntal variations.

Fig. 138a ∧ **Fig. 138b** ∨

Fig. 138c

Schoenberg's Variations for Orchestra Op. 31 is scored for a large orchestra which includes a celesta and mandolins. The basic forms of the series are given in full in Fig. 139. At this point the reader is reminded that the basic sets can also be transposed. Thus

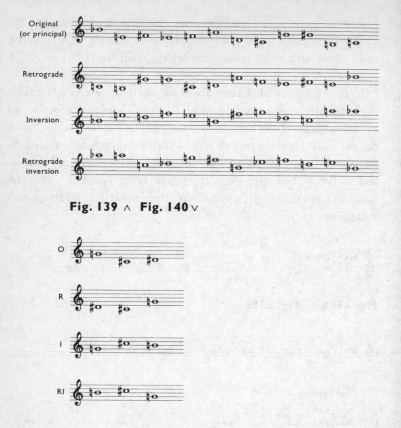

Fig. 139 ∧ **Fig. 140** ∨

if, for the sake of simplicity, we choose the first three notes of the set and start on g♮′ instead of b♭′, we get the notes in transposed original, retrograde, inversion and retrograde inversion (see Fig. 140).

The main theme is twenty-four bars long and is constructed in ternary form (see Fig. 141). The repeated A section is a version of the first twelve bars of the first A shortened to seven bars. The observant reader will notice that the second half of theme A is based on the transposed retrograde inversion of the twelve-note set. (This relationship between the two parts of a melody is called combinatoriality.) Moreover, the return of A is the transposed

Fig. 141

inversion of the set. The B section sandwiched between the two As is the retrograde of the original set.

The whole work consists of an introduction followed by the theme with nine variations and a large-scale finale. In the variations Schoenberg goes through the traditional procedures, that is melodic variation (Var. VII), rhythmic variation (Var. I), harmonic variation (Var. VIII, Var. IV) and special sound effects (Var. IV uses harp, mandolin and celesta, Var. VII piccolo, glockenspiel, celesta and solo violin). But there is something else, which first appeared in the introduction at bars 24–5: a play on the name of Bach. It remains hidden during all the variations, and emerges triumphantly in the finale in several rhythmic forms until its last entry on the trumpet (bars 497–500; see Fig. 142).

Fig. 142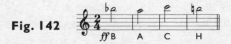

The reader is also recommended to listen to the second movement of Webern's Symphony Op. 21, which consists of a theme, seven variations and a coda.

Passacaglia

The 'ground bass', 'chaconne' and 'passacaglia' are variation techniques that were most popular during the baroque era; the names of Buxtehude, Couperin and, above all, Bach come immediately to mind. Perhaps the most monumental passacaglia written for organ is the Passacaglia in C minor by Bach. Although there are differences between these forms, basically they refer to a repeated melodic–harmonic figure around which the composer unfolds a series of variations.

Of the twentieth-century British composers, it was Britten who had a particular liking for the variation form, to such an extent that he even applied it to his opera *The Turn of the Screw*, a chamber opera in two acts written on a theme and fifteen variations. One of his early works, the Violin Concerto Op. 15, ends with a liberal interpretation of the passacaglia form. A more orthodox example can be found in his opera *Peter Grimes*, where the fourth Interlude linking the first scene with the second scene of Act II is a passacaglia built over the repetition of a theme in the bass (see Fig. 143).

Fig. 143

It is worth noting that Webern's first opus is a passacaglia for orchestra, based on a remarkable theme (see Fig. 144; Fig. 145 is a

Fig. 144

Fig. 145

simplified version of the first variation). This early work, in D minor, is in a late-romantic and expressionistic style. Yet it already shows characteristic features which Webern later developed to the full, such as his preoccupation with variation styles and contrapuntal texture ('Ever different and yet always the same!'): detached notes punctuated by silence, which breaks up the melodic contour and results in a series of short motifs rather than a continuous melodic theme (for example d′–c#′, bb′–ab′, f′–e′); contrapuntal structuring (for example the first three notes, d′ c#′ bb′, are followed by their retrograde inversions, e′ f′ ab′); particular fondness for quiet dynamics (*ppp*, as well as muted instruments); and extreme economy based on contrapuntal motivic thinking (bars 9–16).

The suite

The origin of the suite goes back to the sixteenth century, when it usually comprised two contrasting dances. By the eighteenth century it had become a set of highly stylized dances, of which the most popular were allemande, courante, sarabande and gigue, all in binary form.

In the twentieth-century revival of the baroque musical style modern composers (including Debussy, Ravel, Schoenberg and Berg) tended to resurrect these old dances and adopted them in their own compositions. The term became much more loosely applied by some composers and denoted a set of contrasting pieces – not necessarily dances – which, when put together, presented a unified musical entity (for example, Grieg's *Peer Gynt*, Berg's Lyric Suite and Kodály's *Háry János Suite*). Another way in which the term 'suite' is used is when the music is taken either from a ballet (Stravinsky's suite from *The Firebird*) or from dances of diverse ethnic origins (Milhaud's *Suite provençale*, Bartók's Dance Suite).

Sonata form

Sonata form is one of the great tonality-based structures which evolved during the eighteenth and nineteenth centuries in the hands of Haydn, Mozart, Beethoven, Brahms, Bruckner, Liszt, Mahler and Sibelius, to mention only a selection from the long list of major Western composers who contributed to its development. Its main principle is that of conflict and resolution. The binary, tonal and thematic juxtaposition of dual ideas, or groups of ideas (exposition), is developed and unfolded, sometimes with additional themes (development), before a tonal equilibrium (recapitulation) is regained which concludes the overall ternary structure. The textbook plan, seldom followed to the letter, of classical sonata form is:

Exposition
First subject(s) in tonic key (say, C major)
Second subject(s) in the dominant (G major)

Development
Thematic development, new keys (for example E minor, A
    minor or F major), leading to a climax and then to the

Recapitulation
First subject in tonic key (C major)
Second subject *also* in tonic key (C major)
Coda

As can be seen from this schematic description, the most emphatic *raison d'être* of classical sonata form is the concept of tonal
conflict resolved by a return to tonal equilibrium. With the
weakening or, as is the case with twelve-note compositions, with
the total abandonment of tonality, the very thing that characterizes
the sonata principle has been lost. For this reason it is difficult to
speak about sonata form with reference to modern composition.
All the same, among twentieth-century composers the concept has
been loosely applied in the following main ways:

(a) by adhering roughly to the old sonata principle in establishing
    the subject at least *on* a key, if not *in* a key
(b) by referring to the sonata in the context of its generic meaning
    ('sounding together'), that is, as an instrumental composition as
    opposed to a cantata, which is sung
(c) by using the sonata principle in 'progressive tonality': when a
    composition is in one key at the beginning and ends in a
    different key
(d) by means of the ingenious application of the form within the
    twelve-note system
(e) by means of a highly idiosyncratic process of thematic and
    harmonic organization giving the semblance of sonata
    structure

It is debatable whether one can still talk about sonata form with regard to the last two. It may be possible only by analogy.

Bartók, whose synthesis-oriented approach to music led him to adhere to and revitalize classical forms, gives us a memorable example of sonata form in the second movement of his *Music for Strings, Percussion and Celesta*. As the last note of the first movement was A, at the beginning of the second movement Bartók leaps up to C via A, but from bar 7 he moves to the tonic key of C from the orthodox dominant G, firmly establishing the first subject of the exposition (see Fig. 146). The second subject (there are four themes within this subject, but the first is sufficient to make the point) appears on the dominant (see Fig. 147). All this

Fig. 146 ∧ **Fig. 147** ∨

material leads to the development, which begins on a C♯ at bar 167. This section contains great contrapuntal and rhythmical ingenuity, and a fugue starts at bar 310 (see Fig. 148). The point of recapitulation (bar 372) is characterized by rapid metric changes

Fig. 148

(see Fig. 149). The second subject appears again, but now on C (see Fig. 150). The themes belonging to the second subject group are also recapitulated, and finally lead to the coda at bar 490; the movement reaches its end at bar 520 firmly on C.

Fig. 149 ∧ **Fig. 150** ∨

There is, of course, much more to this movement than what has been described here. But the aim of the above was to see to what extent the grand design of sonata form was a discernible reality. Would Mozart or Beethoven have been able to recognize, after the initial shock, the sonata form in Bartók's music? The answer is probably yes, as it contains all the classical characteristics of the form they themselves practised with such skill.

Before venturing further, the reader is reminded that musical forms represent archetypal patterns applicable to other media. At first glance one would not necessarily link, say, cake-making and architecture with composition. Yet there is a structural relationship. Fig. 151 presents a set of visual analogies which, it is hoped, will make the abstract nature of musical patterns more concrete.

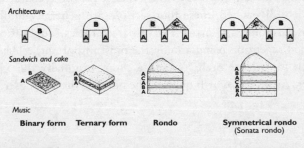

Architecture

Sandwich and cake

Music

Binary form   **Ternary form**   **Rondo**   **Symmetrical rondo**
(Sonata rondo)

Fig. 151

The symphony

Sonata form was a major ingredient in the composition of larger-scale works – the string quartet, symphony, concerto and sonata itself. The sonata (as opposed to sonata form) refers to an instrumental composition which in general consists of three or four contrasting movements. Sonata form was the usual structure for the first movement, and is therefore sometimes referred to as first movement form. This is misleading, as sonata form can be used for any one or all of the movements. Broadly speaking, the symphony is a sonata for orchestra, even in its various modern manifestations.

During this century the symphony, being so deeply rooted in the diatonic system and the application of sonata form, was usually practised by those composers who, in one way or another, adhered to tonality, such as Sibelius, Stravinsky (until he defected to atonality), Shostakovich, Prokofiev and Vaughan Williams. The atonal composers made less use of the form. Berg's *Wozzeck* is a largely atonal opera which incorporates the idea of the symphony as part of its structure in Act II. Webern's single essay in this form, the Symphony Op. 21, is hardly a symphony, except in the sense of 'sounding together'. It contains two movements, of which the first (for four voices) is a highly elaborate canonic work in contrary motion. The second movement, as mentioned earlier, is based on a theme, seven variations and a coda. Berio's *Sinfonia*, though written in four movements or sections (later extended to five), is far removed from the classical symphony; the composer himself, however, said that while 'their expressive characters are extremely diversified, these four sections are generally unified by similar harmonic and articulatory characteristics (duplication and extended repetition being among the most important)'. The *Sinfonia* calls for a large orchestra and a choir, originally the Swingle Singers. Again it is worth quoting the notes of the composer:

I The text of the first part consists of a series of short fragments from *Le Cru et le cuit* by the French anthropologist Claude Lévi-Strauss. These fragments are taken from a section of the book which analyses the structure and symbology of Brazilian myths about the origins of water and related myths characterized by similar structure.

II The second section of *Sinfonia* is a tribute to the memory of Dr Martin Luther King. Here the vocal part is based on his name, nothing else.

III The main text for the third section includes excerpts from Samuel Beckett's *The Unnameable*, which in turn prompts a selection from many other sources, including Joyce, spoken phrases of Harvard undergraduates, slogans written by the students on the Sorbonne walls during last May's [1968] insurrection in Paris (at which I was present), recorded dialogues with my friends and family, snatches of solfège and so on.

IV The text for the fourth section, a sort of coda, is based on a short selection from those used in the three preceding parts.

The third section is the most complex and longest of the four. In addition to the sources named by the composer above, the section contains quotations from other composers' works, from Bach to Stockhausen and 'beyond'. But the main and unifying quotation on which the section is based comes from the third movement of Mahler's Second Symphony. Mahler's scherzo is seen by Berio as 'a container within whose framework a large number of references are proliferated, interrelated and integrated into the following structure of the original work itself'. Thus what we have is something of a collage or, rather, an *objet trouvé*. Mahler, we are told, is to music what Beckett is to text, an unfolding stream of consciousness which Berio likened to the image of a river. The *Sinfonia*, above all the third section, is one of the most original expressions of the symphonic idea of the 1960s.

Although it is not immediately apparent, Peter Maxwell Davies's Symphony No. 2 is tonal. It is in B minor, and the E♯ in it functions as an alternative dominant instead of the traditionally expected F♯; this interval guarantees tension as it is a tritone (augmented fourth or diminished fifth). The composer has been quick to explain: 'there is here no easy return to old tonality – I feel there can be no short cuts to a new musical simplicity by these means, but that tonality might be extended to furnish new methods of cohesion'. Thus the halfway point in the octave from B is not F♯ as in the traditional tonal thinking but E♯, which is introduced as an exact 'geographical' halfway between the two poles. (Bartók experimented with this method in the first movement of his Music for Strings, Percussion and Celesta.) The traditional four-movement structure of the symphony is not altered by Davies in his first three symphonies. The finale of his Symphony No. 2 echoes the passacaglia idea of Brahms's Symphony No. 4, albeit in an episodic form.

These symphonies also show that the fundamentally romantic nature of Davies, which often hides behind parody and the grotesque, has gained the upper hand in his musical thinking. It seems that we are witnessing not so much parody but a creative synthesis in which, through his symphonies, the European history of music from the time of the Gregorian chant to the present is given form in monumental sound edifices. That is why Davies has returned to the symphony and also, through his re-evaluation of this form, to Bruckner, Mahler and Sibelius. Symphony No. 3 is the summation of this phase. Its first movement (Lento – Allegro alla breve) opens with a slow introductory section which starts with a drumroll and establishes the tonal–modal point of D; as in Symphony No. 2, the characteristic diminished fifth appears (see Fig. 152). The thematic material is based on plainsong. The second

Fig. 152

movement (Scherzo I – Allegro) and the third (Scherzo II – Allegro vivace) are linked as a structural whole within the outer movements and are further related by use of similar materials. The composer has explained his musical intentions by analogy:

it is as if one experiences some musical equivalent of a nave, where the eye progresses towards the altar from a fixed central point with all the proportions revealed and the sidechapels partly exposed, throughout the second movement, and with a disturbed experience of the same seen from a side arcade in the third – i.e. the vantage point is no longer static. I have interrupted the third movement by letting in 'windows', which, towards its conclusion, and taking the place of a 'trio', open out to give brief glimpses towards the finale – a device I have shamelessly borrowed from the 'Burlesque' of Mahler's Ninth Symphony, which also concludes with a slow movement.

In the finale (Lento) the music expands and reaches its grandiose climax and resolution.

No, the symphony is not dead as we have been led to believe on occasions; it is still with us. True, it is sometimes reduced to its etymological meaning, or it appears in highly modified ways and bears little resemblance to its original four-movement structure. But since the 1970s there seems to have been a slow return to its traditional format, albeit, as is the case with Davies, by synthesis and free reinterpretation of the model.

It was Beethoven who, in his Ninth Symphony in D minor, introduced the idea of blending the symphony with solo and choral singing. This was later taken up by Liszt (*Faust Symphony*) and Mahler, who amalgamated the German lieder with the symphonic idea in, for example, his Symphony No. 4 in G Major and *Das Lied von der Erde*. Shostakovich, a Mahlerite to such an extent that his friends suggested he was suffering from Mahleria, carried the song-symphony further in his Symphony No. 14, where the eleven sections are all symphonic song settings.

The concerto

The overall form of the concerto seems to have been largely undisturbed by modern developments. The three-movement pattern Fast – Slow – Fast is still the most popular.

The one-movement concerto, in which the different movements are telescoped into a continuous single movement, was taken up by Ravel in his Piano Concerto for the left hand. Another new development is the blending of the cadenza with the general flow of the concerto by accompanying it instead of letting it be a solo bravura part, as occurs in Berg's Violin Concerto.

The concerto grosso

With the returned interest in the musical forms of the baroque period, the idea of the concerto grosso was reintroduced by such modern composers as Krenek, Hindemith, Stravinsky and Bartók. In a concerto grosso a small group of instruments (called *concertino* or *principale*) plays in combination with a larger body of instruments, the full orchestra (called *tutti* or *ripieno*). A new concerto genre grew out of the concerto grosso principle, the concerto for orchestra, in which the composer gives a virtuoso display not so much to a solo or small solo group as to the whole modern orchestra. The main reason for this is likely to be the virtuoso development of the orchestra and orchestral sections, which enabled composers to apply the concerto grosso idea to the totality of a large symphony orchestra. Outstanding examples in the repertory are Hindemith's Concerto for Orchestra Op. 38, Piston's Concerto for Orchestra, Bartók's Concerto for Orchestra, Gerhard's Concerto for Orchestra, Tippett's Concerto for Orchestra and Lutosławski's Concerto for Orchestra. The list is impressive.

The individual movements of the solo concerto, concerto grosso or concerto for orchestra may take any one or a combination of the larger forms or textures already mentioned.

Chamber music: the string quartet

The forms and textures discussed in this and earlier chapters are equally applicable to chamber compositions. It should be remembered that when more than one or two instruments are involved these are named trio, quartet, quintet and so on. Thus a quartet is normally a sonata for four string instruments: first and second violins, viola and cello. There are, of course, exceptions, among them Messiaen's *Quatuor pour la fin du temps*, which is for piano, clarinet, violin and cello. Moreover, its structuring is based not on the old principle of the sonata, but on a series of programmatic tableaux. Although in common parlance the noun 'quartet' is used to mean a string quartet, for the sake of clarity it is preferable to use the latter.

Even taking into account the notable exceptions in string quartet writing, such as Stravinsky's Three Pieces for string quartet, Webern's Six Bagatelles Op. 9 and String Quartet Op. 28, Ives's First and Second String Quartets, Cage's String Quartet and Boulez's *Livre pour quatuor*, the string quartet style has sustained a relatively traditional profile which maintains the dichotomy of sophisticated entertainment and highly intimate, quasi-self-revelatory musical utterances handed down by Haydn, Mozart and, above all, Beethoven and Schubert. This tendency is made evident in the string quartets of Bartók, Schoenberg, Shostakovich, Britten, Tippett, Piston and Carter, to pick out only a few names from the rich treasure-house of twentieth-century chamber music.

Vocal styles

We turn now to vocal compositions. In setting a text to music there are, of course, several options. In fact, any of the forms we have examined could be used in vocal music as well, but some texts suggest their own particular forms. There is, nevertheless, a

Fig. 153

distinct choice to make when writing a song: whether it should be 'strophic' or 'through-composed'.

Strophic form

A song is in strophic form when every stanza of the text is set to the same or nearly the same music. Gershwin's famous 'Summertime' (see Fig. 153), for instance, starts with a piano introduction which leads to a song of two stanzas with an identical melody and accompaniment. The song ends with a coda characterized by a chromatic sequential chord progression and a repeated section of the melody played in the bass.

Through-composed song

A through-composed song (German *durchkomponiert*) is the opposite of a strophic song in that, as its name implies, for every stanza of the text there is new music. Whereas a strophic song gives a sense of unity and quick familiarity, allowing the listener to follow the text, a through-composed song grants the composer greater dramatic freedom to reflect the various contrasting nuances in the text. Fig. 154 quotes the opening two bars in each stanza of Bartók's 'New Hungarian Folksong' (*Mikrokosmos* Vol. V No. 127).

Fig. 154a

Now a lone bird seeks her mates - so mourn-ful - ly.

cresc.

Fig. 154b ∧ **Fig. 154c** ∨

a tempo

High a-bove the corn a lark now earth-ward flies.

f

Still she mourns the mate who left her lone-ly here.

cresc.

f

Fig. 154d

Speech-melody

It is by no means an overstatement to say that songwriting has flourished during this century, even when comparing it with the vogue of the nineteenth-century Austro-German lieder. One could argue that in general terms the reliance on text so prominent in serial and other avant-garde musical compositions gave a cohesive comprehensibility to many compositions which would otherwise have been more difficult for the public to understand. Webern is a revealing example. Out of his thirty-one numbered opuses nineteen are text-based vocal compositions; of those without opus numbers about thirteen are vocal. In each case more than half of his compositions are oriented towards text and voice. In Schoenberg's much larger output vocal music also takes up a substantial proportion of the whole. Furthermore, whether we look at the works of the lyrical Dallapiccola, the dadaist–surrealist Kagel or some of the minimalists, texts set to music or quite simply extramusical programmatic ideas, whatever these may be, have been and are inspiring twentieth-century composers in a striking fashion. It is difficult to say whether this embracing of the extra-musical is an overflow from the nineteenth century – the Mahlerian fusion of the lieder and symphony, Wagner's fusion of the arts – or whether it is perhaps a much more pragmatic substitution for the loss of tonality (key centre): the text becomes the unifying element and point of reference in a musical context which to this day baffles the average listener. One thing is certain, that in the works of several modern composers poetry, drama and music were united, yet again, in order to express the human condition.

It is not by chance that Schoenberg's revolutionary notions found expression in his setting of fifteen poems by Stefan George, *Das Buch der hängenden Gärten* Op. 15. Two of these songs, 'Litanei' and 'Entrückung', were set for soprano and string quartet in his Second String Quartet in F♯ minor. The setting of 'Entrückung' in the finale led Schoenberg not only to atonality, but also to a new vocal style, a speechlike recitation of great declamatory intensity: 'speech-melody'. Singing was never to be the same again. Ironically, the idea first appeared in Humperdinck's opera *Königskinder* near the end of the nineteenth century. Humperdinck, known mainly for his opera *Hänsel und Gretel*, discarded it just at the time when Schoenberg fully adopted it for the projection of atonal expressionistic frenzy. The best known of all the pieces written in this style must be *Pierrot lunaire*, which Schoenberg based on the setting of twenty-one (a cycle of 7 × 3 songs) poems by Albert Giraud in German translation. These 'melodramas', as Schoenberg liked to refer to them, are accompanied by a small chamber ensemble that includes a piano. The work is highly contrapuntal, consisting of canons, fugue, passacaglias and so on, and within the context of atonal expressionism ranges from grotesque, nightmarish hallucination to melancholy. With *Pierrot* the image of alienation, the sad figure of the outsider as a clown, was firmly established in music as well. Generally for speech-melody the music is written normally but with an added ' × ' sign on the stems (see Fig. 155), which indicates the immediate fall or rise of the voice away from the notes. The overall effect is ethereal, perfectly suiting the imagery of the moonstruck Pierrot.

Fig. 155

There are three German terms describing the above singing style in current use: *Sprechgesang* (speech-song), *Sprechstimme* (speech-voice), *Sprechmelodie* (speech-melody).

Choral works

Larger-scale choral forms from earlier periods (the seventeenth and eighteenth centuries), among them the cantata, oratorio, passion and requiem, also had a modest comeback. Honegger's *Cantate de Noël*, *Cris du monde* and *Jeanne d'Arc au bûcher*, Penderecki's *St Luke Passion* and *Polish Requiem*, Bartók's *Cantata profana* and the majestic *War Requiem* of Britten are outstanding examples of this revival.

Opera

For years one was told that opera, like sonata form and the symphony, was dead, or at least in a terminal state. This has been most powerfully refuted by such composers as Britten, Birtwistle, Davies, Henze, Ligeti, Stockhausen, Philip Glass and John Adams. Opera is still a living genre, and long may it last.

Apart from Debussy's symbolistic operatic masterpiece, *Pelléas et Mélisande*, one of the most important developments in opera was the appliance and absorption of atonal as well as serial techniques. Berg's two operas, *Wozzeck* and *Lulu*, provide us with fascinating examples. As far as the subject-matter is concerned, Berg, with relentless psychological logic, adheres to the expressionist preoccupations with alienation, victimization, the social misfit, jealousy, madness, murder, sexual degradation, prostitution and so on. These cardinal themes of expressionist thinking are all brought together in his two operas.

In the music of *Wozzeck* both atonal and tonal elements are ingeniously combined within a formal symphonic framework that is executed with extraordinary rigour. Seldom has there been a more congenial encounter of minds than Büchner's and Berg's. The fate of the victimized soldier and his mistress is sealed from the moment the curtain is raised. What one hears and sees in a state of compassionate terror is the unfolding of the inevitable tragedy. The score is a mine of technical displays based on most forms in the repertory. Its plan is so fascinating that it is given in Tables 1–3 in full. (By looking at the right-hand column one can see the musical forms used by Berg for every scene in this three-act opera.)

Lulu is based on another playwright's work, Wedekind's *Erdgeist* and *Die Büchse der Pandora*, and concerns the rise and fall of a sensually oriented woman, a 'wild beast'. This opera is serial. As we saw on p. 49 (Fig. 63), Berg derived a harmonic sequence of four three-note chords from the twelve-note set. Lulu's themes – the two sides of her, as it were – are constructed out of these chords (see Fig. 156); the second is the inversion of the first.

Fig. 156a ∧ **Fig. 156b** ∨

As with *Wozzeck*, the outline of the dramatic and musical layout of the three acts of *Lulu* was carefully planned. In a letter to Schoenberg Berg wrote:

Since I have been obliged to cut four-fifths of Wedekind's original text, the difficulty lies in knowing what to retain in the remaining fifth. And it is only increased if I try to subordinate everything to the musical forms (large and small) and still preserve Wedekind's individual language . . . Anyway, although these problems of detail have been troublesome, I have long ago decided on a general plan for transforming the play into an

Table 1 ACT I *Wozzeck and the surrounding world (exposition) – five character studies*

Scene	Time and place of action	Characters	Musical forms
Scene 1	The Captain's room; early morning	Wozzeck and the Captain	'The Captain' Suite: Prelude, Pavan, Cadenza, Gigue, Cadenza, Gavotte Double I/II, Air, Prelude in form of retrogression
Scene 2	An open field, the town in the distance; late afternoon	Wozzeck and Andres	'Andres' Rhapsody on a sequence of three chords and the three-verse hunting song of Andres
Scene 3	Marie's room; evening	Marie, Margret and the child; later Wozzeck	'Marie' Military march Lullaby
Scene 4	The Doctor's study; sunny afternoon	Wozzeck and the Doctor	'The Doctor' Passacaglia (chaconne); twelve-note theme with twenty-one variations
Scene 5	Street before Marie's door; evening twilight	Marie and the Drum Major	'The Drum Major' Andante affettuoso (rondo)

Table 2 ACT II *Dramatic development (denouement) – symphony in five movements*

Scene	Time and place of action	Characters	Musical forms
Scene 1	Marie's room; morning sunshine	Marie and the child; later Wozzeck	Sonata movement: exposition (main, subsidiary and final themes), first reprise, development, second reprise
Scene 2	Street in town; daytime	The Captain and the Doctor; later Wozzeck	Fantasy and fugue on three themes
Scene 3	Street before Marie's door; a dull day	Marie and Wozzeck	Largo (a chamber orchestra in the instrumentation of Arnold Schoenberg's Chamber Symphony)
Scene 4	Tavern garden; late evening	Apprentices, soldiers and girls, first and second apprentices, Andres, the Drum Major and Marie; a little later Wozzeck; finally the madman	Scherzo: Scherzo I (ländler), Trio I (song of the second apprentice), Scherzo II (waltz), Trio II (huntsmen's chorus of the apprentices and Andres's song), Scherzo I (ländler in a varied form), Trio I (song in a varied form upon the prayer of the second apprentice), Scherzo II (waltz with development)

| Scene 5 | Guardroom in the barracks; right | Soldiers, Wozzeck and Andres; later the Drum Major | Rondo martiale con introduzione |

Table 3 ACT III *Catastrophe – six inventions*

Scene	*Time and place of action*	*Characters*	*Musical forms*
Scene 1	Marie's room; night: candlelight	Marie and the child	Invention on a theme: theme, seven variations and fugue
Scene 2	Forest path by a pool; dusk is falling	Wozzeck and Marie	Invention on one tone (B)
Scene 3	A low tavern; night, badly lit	Apprentices, girls, Wozzeck and Margret	Invention on a rhythm
Scene 4	Forest path by a pool; moonlit night	Wozzeck; later the Captain and the Doctor	Invention on a sixth chord Invention on a key
Scene 5	Street before Marie's door; bright morning: sunshine	Marie's child, other children	Invention on a quaver rhythm

opera. This involves musical as well as dramatic proportions, and most of all the scenario, which looks like this:

The two plays		The opera
Erdgeist	Act I – Painter's studio, in which Dr Goll, Lulu's husband, dies of a stroke	Act I (three scenes)
	Act II – The apartment of Lulu and her second husband, the painter, who commits suicide	
	Act III – The dressing room of Lulu, now a dancer, whom Schoen promises to marry	
	Act IV – Schoen's apartment, where he is killed by Lulu. She is arrested	Act II (two scenes divided by a long interval)
Die Büchse der Pandora	After one year in prison, Lulu is released by the Countess Geschwitz and returns to	(In Berg, one year in prison)
	Act I – Schoen's apartment (same set as before). She becomes Alwa's mistress	
	Act II – Gambling club in Paris. Lulu has to escape	Act III (two scenes)
	Act III – A London attic	

By means of paying my respect to both parties you see how (in my Act II) I have brought together the parts that are separate in Wedekind; there are two plays there. The interlude by which I have joined the last act of *Erdgeist* and the first of *Die Büchse der Pandora* is actually the pivotal point of the tragedy, as it is there that the rise of the first part is replaced by the fall of the second.

The basic row is not used thematically in the opera until Act II, when Lulu sings an aria which is the central point of the opera (see Fig. 157).

Wenn sich die Men-schen um   mei - net-wil-len   um-ge-bracht ha-ben,

Fig. 157

It is natural that the compositional sophistication displayed in these operas should be fascinating. Berg, nevertheless, warned listeners that 'however well one may know how much logic has gone into the working-out of the compositions, no matter how much clever equipment may be hidden in each single detail . . . from the moment the curtain rises to the moment when the curtain comes down at the end . . . no one should want to be concerned with anything except the opera itself'. What Berg is calling for is the conscious practice of creative innocence in order to retain the freshness of an artistic experience.

The aspects of forms and textures discussed and illustrated in this chapter should go some way towards equipping the reader with an understanding of certain technicalities, which should be of help when a piece is being performed. Berg's advice, however, should be borne in mind.

CHAPTER FOUR

New Musical Ideas, New Ways of Using Instruments: *old and new instruments, modern orchestration,* musique concrète, *electronic music, computer music*

Instrumentation is, in music, the exact equivalent of colour in painting.

HECTOR BERLIOZ

CRAFT: What is good instrumentation?
STRAVINSKY: When you are unaware that it is instrumentation.

IGOR STRAVINSKY

In this chapter we will not be dealing with what may be called the rudiments of instruments and the orchestra, that is, the description of standard instruments, their range and general use. A basic knowledge of these is taken for granted; any reader who requires more detail is advised to consult the relevant chapter in *Introducing Music* and to turn to the recommended books on instruments and instrumentation in its Bibliography. The aim here is to examine in general what has happened to the orchestra since Debussy's time, and in particular to look at the new ways in which old instruments are used. Some new developments, including aspects of electronic music, will also be considered.

There are two fundamental topics concerning instruments and the orchestra: the grouping of instruments from the point of view of their voice range; the dissolution of the standard orchestra.

Standard grouping

The orchestra and the subdivision of instruments into groups within it show the influence of vocal origins and tradition in that the ranges of the human voice are followed both individually and in groups: soprano, alto, tenor and bass. Accordingly, we find that the orchestra is divided into four main groups: woodwind, brass, percussion and strings. To a fifth category belong those instruments which are not normally part of the first four. Here is a list of those sections, working from the lowest (bass) to the highest (soprano):

Woodwind
Without reeds: bass flute, alto flute, flute, piccolo
With single reeds: clarinets: bass (B♭), alto (E♭), soprano (B♭ and
    A); saxophones: bass, baritone, tenor, alto, soprano
With double reeds: contrabassoon, bassoon, English horn, oboe

Brass
Tuba, trombone, cornet, trumpet, horn

Timpani and percussion
With definite pitch: timpani, chimes, glockenspiel, xylophone,
    marimba, celesta, vibraphone
With indefinite pitch: bass drum, side drum (snare drum), cymbals,
    tambourine, triangle, castanets, gong, etc.

Strings
Double bass, violoncello, viola, first and second violins

Extra instruments
Harp, piano, organ, etc.

From examining this list it is quite apparent that if one applies the human voice division already referred to, all the instruments will fit into one of the four specific categories. Under the heading 'soprano', for instance, the following instruments could be put together: violin (first), trumpet (first), saxophone (soprano), clarinet in B♭, oboe, flute and piccolo.

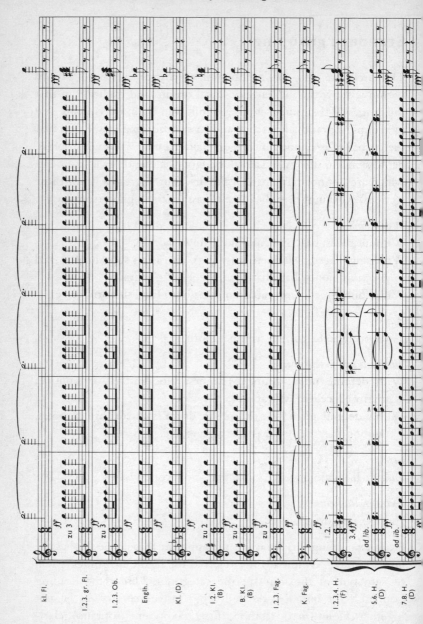

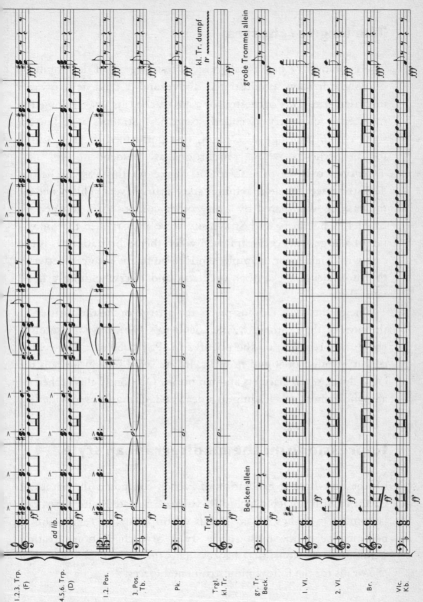

Fig. 158

The large orchestra

The evolution of orchestral music shows a gradual development of standardization as illustrated above and a tendency towards increased size. This orchestral obesity reached its peak during the nineteenth and early twentieth centuries. Strauss's well-known score of *Till Eulenspiegel* Op. 28, first performed in 1895, called for an orchestra whose proportions are evident in Fig. 158. Twenty-two types of instruments make up this vast orchestra. The string section alone requires sixty-four players. This penchant for vastness was shared by many other composers of the period: Mahler, Schoenberg and Stravinsky were all partial to the sonorities of a large-scale orchestra even when the orchestration, as is the case with Mahler for example, tends to be finely balanced between the most delicate chamber orchestra and overwhelmingly large *tutti* effects.

One of the most famous pieces for a large orchestra, written at the turn of the century, was Schoenberg's *Gurrelieder* for soloists, choir and orchestra, on the poems of J. P. Jacobsen, a nineteenth-century Danish poet and novelist. In the wind section he calls for eight flutes, seven clarinets and ten horns. Obviously this orchestral aggrandizement was leading to a dead end: change was inevitable.

Impressionism: the Mediterranean style

Of the post-Berlioz generation of French composers the names of Chabrier, Fauré, Debussy and Ravel are associated with a particular timbre in orchestration. Debussy's impressionist tone-painting became one of the most subtle styles of orchestration, creating sensuous and colouristic nuances. The *Prélude à l'après-midi d'un faune* calls for the following instrumental forces:

3 flutes	2 bassoons	Violin I
2 oboes	4 horns	Violin II
1 English horn	2 harps	Viola
2 clarinets	Antique cymbals	Cello
		Double bass

This is by no means excessive. Debussy never used a large orchestra for the purpose of obtaining forceful volumes. What is telling here is the choice of three flutes, one English horn, two harps and a pair of antique cymbals. If we now look at the first fourteen bars of the full score (see Fig. 159), we notice the tempo indication 'Très modéré (M.M. ♩ = 44)'; a solo flute plays a sensuous chromatic melody, the dynamic is *p* and the flautist is to be 'doux et expressif'; the woodwind enter at bar 4, giving harmonic support above a glissando played on the first harp. Until the end of bar 4 the rest of the orchestra is silent. At bar 5 the second harp enters, together with double bass, divisi cellos and viola, between them playing a Bb major seventh chord; the time signature has changed from 9/8 to 6/8; the dynamic is now even softer, *pp*; the strings are all muted; the first and third horns play their languishing little motifs in turn, as if awakening; at bar 6 there is total silence . . . Later, at bar 11, the strings play a tremolo under the solo flute, giving a shimmering effect.

Already in its first bars the score contains several features typical of Debussy's compositional thinking. The music is suggestive rather than dialectic or rhetorical; neither the melody nor the harmony shares the Teutonically regulated inner drive of melodic phrasing and harmonic progression; the melody quickly gives way to fragmentation and short atmospheric motifs using muted, divisi strings and tremolo. The French predilection for the sound of the harp (above all the use of glissando), soft dynamics, silence and static, long-held notes gives this music a peculiar individuality characterized by understatement rather than the extrovert aggression which is a dominating part of Strauss's orchestral palette.

Fig. 159

Fig. 159 contd.

Regardless of the fact that Debussy's interest in fine art was marginal, the convenient label 'impressionist', borrowed from that field, stuck to him. His music could be related to symbolist poetry and drama with even more justification, as he was more at home in literature. Stylistically he was as much of a symbolist as an impressionist. His music drama *Pelléas et Mélisande*, based on the text of a play by Maeterlinck, a symbolist poet and dramatist, is one of those superb works whose poetic text and music meet in terms of style and technique. Maeterlinck's characters are introverted poetic souls who communicate through largely fragmented statements of deep symbolic significance. The obscure greenhouse atmosphere of refined unreality suited Debussy perfectly. This opera is the apotheosis of his orchestral style. For most of the composition only a small section of the orchestra plays, thus creating a delicately subdued chamber orchestra effect. Although influenced by Wagner (Debussy to a certain extent borrowed the idea of the 'leitmotif'), his Pelléas (see Fig. 160) could hardly be further from Wagner's Tristan.

Fig. 160

Fig. 161

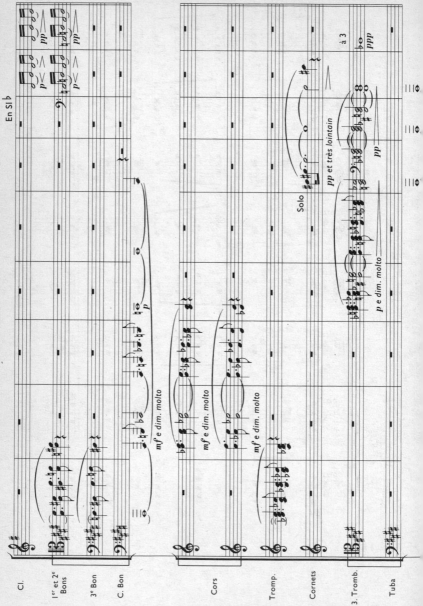

Fig. 162

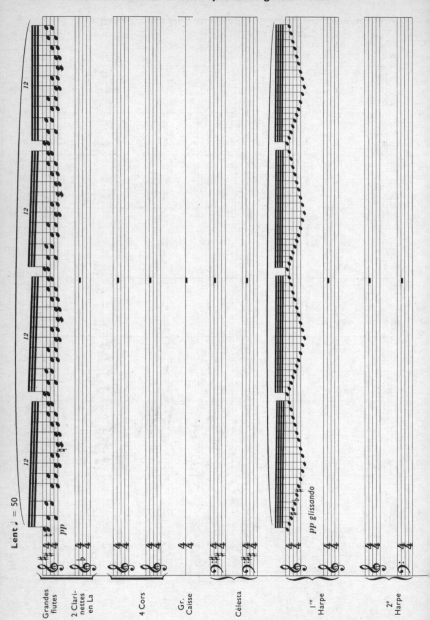

Fig. 163

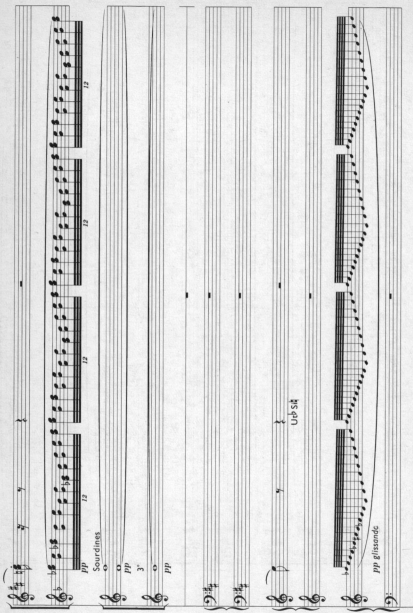

Fig. 163 contd.

Diaghilev commissioned Debussy to write a ballet based on the choreography of Nijinsky. The story of *Jeux* concerns two girls and a young man's casual encounter, and their playing a game of tennis in the night. The shadowy nocturnal scene of sport, flirtation and a subdued yet dominating sexuality that engenders a risqué *ménage-à-trois* atmosphere is interrupted by the unexpected fall of a tennis ball; the frivolous threesome run away, leaving the viewer to wonder what all this is about. The music, which was unfortunately overshadowed by the first performance of Stravinsky's *Rite of Spring* in 1913, is one of Debussy's most daring compositions. It is characterized by the unfolding of motifs which appear and disappear in a continuous variational flow, pointing to later twentieth-century developments. The score gains its originality from the subtle orchestration, with its special effects for strings and woodwind. This is further emphasized by his use of polytonality and rhythmic variety with frequent rubatos.

In Debussy's orchestral homage to the Mediterranean world, *Ibéria*, the Spanish guitar is evoked on divisi strings with a masterful brushstroke of colours and rhythm (see Fig. 161).

In *La Mer* the double bassoon gives depth below the shimmering string tremolos, the chorus of four horns is echoed by the three trombones playing in closed position (as the French preferred), while the cornet plays a short awakening motif *pp et très lointain* (see Fig. 162). Like the impressionist painters, Debussy's orchestral palette gives us the illusion of 'plein air', of distance and light, but, above all, of colour.

Ravel's prodigious orchestral technique is well known through his orchestration of Mussorgsky's *Pictures at an Exhibition*. All his works – *Boléro*, *La Valse*, *Daphnis et Chloé*, *L'Enfant et les sortilèges*, the String Quartet in F, the Piano Concerto for the left hand and so on – whether written for orchestra, opera or chamber ensemble, display superb technical command and imagination. Some composers possess a particular quality which can be encapsulated in a word. With Elgar, for instance, this word is 'nobilmente'; with Ravel it is 'enchantment'. Most of his music relies on extra-

musical ideas taken from antiquity, fairy tales and the Mediterranean world, especially Spain. These, as well as evocative old and
modern dances, are metamorphosed into his 'enchanted garden',
which he quietly cultivated to such perfection. In spite of the
differences between Debussy and Ravel, their orchestral palettes
can be very similar on occasions, as may be heard in the passage
from *Daphnis et Chloé* in Fig. 163. The impressionist oscillation is
there in the orchestration as it is in his earlier Liszt-influenced
piano composition *Jeux d'eau* (see Fig. 164).

Fig. 164

In his only String Quartet, on the other hand, he displays a
classical transparency of texture in which a graceful modal and
tonal world is moulded into the overall sonata structure of the
first movement. In Fig. 165 the second subject enters on the first
violin and viola. It is not neoclassicism, but classicism, which was
as natural to Ravel as was his so-called artificiality. As he himself
said with irony, 'I am naturally artificial.'

Fig. 165

From large to small chamber orchestra

It is customary to date the sudden change in fashion from large to chamber orchestra from Schoenberg's Chamber Symphony No. 1 Op. 9, scored for fifteen instrumentalists and completed in 1906. Like the First Quartet Op. 7, in D minor, the Chamber Symphony's four movements are interlocked and played throughout without the usual pauses between movements. Its harmony is largely built on fourths, and the melody too is derived from this interval. As so often with Schoenberg, the score looks conventional, but sounds strikingly different (see Fig. 166). The overall structure of this composition is fascinating, as Schoenberg arranged the sonata form across the continuous flow of the four movements in the following way:

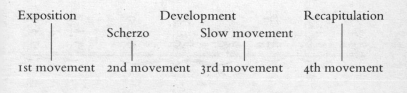

Exposition		Development		Recapitulation
	Scherzo		Slow movement	
1st movement	2nd movement	3rd movement	4th movement	

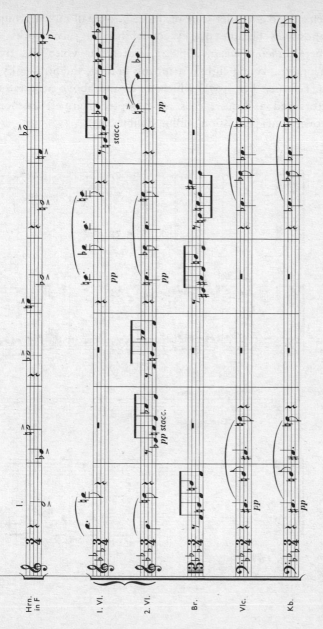

Fig. 166

The change to a smaller scale or, indeed, to small mixed groups of compositions became quickly established in such works as Schoenberg's *Pierrot lunaire* Op. 21, scored for voice and five instrumentalists playing eight instruments in total, and Stravinsky's *Soldier's Tale* (see Fig. 167), which, over and above a narrator, two actors and a dancer, calls for a septet (clarinet, bassoon, cornet, trombone, percussion, violin, double bass).

Fig. 167

The disintegration of the standard orchestra

From the time of Mozart onwards it was taken for granted that the orchestra consisted of strings, percussion (timpani), brass and woodwind; the main 'burden' rested on the strings, especially the violins. To leave the violins, for example, out of an orchestral or symphonic work was unheard of. Yet that is what happened in several twentieth-century cases, of which the best known is Stravinsky's Symphony of Psalms, where the violins are omitted.

The title of his Symphonies of Wind Instruments speaks for itself. It is, however, not a symphony, but a series of 'litanies', as Stravinsky called the sections within his composition, for the groupings of the wind instruments. The reference to symphony should be understood in its etymological sense, that is, 'sounding together' (see Fig. 168).

Honegger scored his Symphony No. 2 for strings alone, but when the first violins play a chorale in the scherzo finale of this three-movement symphony, a trumpet joins them, leading the music to an uplifting close. Webern's Symphony Op. 21 is scored for a small orchestra consisting of clarinet, bass clarinet, two French horns, harp and strings without double basses.

One could carry on listing composition after composition in which the scoring shows a clear break from the traditional format. It is hoped that the examples given here illustrate the striking changes which have taken place in this century. Since about 1910 the term 'orchestra' has been used by composers with great flexibility in connection with works which range from chamber to large-scale symphonic proportions and in which instrumental sections are omitted or replaced or have their roles swapped. In sum, the fixed images of the classical and romantic orchestras have largely disappeared.

Fig. 168

The inclusion of unusual sound effects

For colouristic and atmospheric reasons, several composers have chosen to introduce sound effects into their works which fall into the following categories:

(a) instruments outside the general norm
(b) exotic instruments
(c) new sounds from voices and standard instruments
(d) musical use of extra-musical sound-making sources
(e) new instruments

We will now discuss and illustrate these in turn.

(a) Instruments outside the general norm

Mandolin The mandolin, a plucked string instrument with four double strings tuned to g d′ a′ e″, became popular as a melodic instrument, often with a guitar accompaniment, during the eighteenth and early nineteenth centuries, and gained an entry into the operatic repertory (for instance Arne's *Almona* and Mozart's *Don Giovanni*). Although almost entirely forgotten, it was resurrected in the early twentieth century by Mahler in *Das Lied von der Erde*, Webern in Five Pieces for orchestra Op. 10, Schoenberg in Variations for Orchestra Op. 31 and Stravinsky in *Agon* (see Fig. 169), to mention a few well-known examples.

Guitar The guitar, another plucked string instrument, has six strings tuned to E A d g b e′. Its distinguished history goes back to the thirteenth century as far as western Europe is concerned, as it was then that it appeared in Spain, arguably from Greek via Arabic sources. It became very popular in the Spanish peninsula, reaching its golden age during the seventeenth and eighteenth centuries. By the middle of the nineteenth century, not unlike the mandolin, it had fallen out of fashion; it continued to be used in

Fig. 169

folk music, however. With Francisco Tárrega's and others' dedicated enthusiasm, the guitar came to prominence again during the latter part of the nineteenth century and in the early twentieth. By now, of course, the guitar is known mostly in the context of popular music, but the classical guitar revival headed by Segovia and other more recent performers, such as Julian Bream and John Williams, has firmly secured a place for it in the concert repertory.

Again we find Mahler to be among the first to utilize the sound of the guitar in a late-romantic score, his Seventh Symphony, written in 1904–5. Other distinguished examples are Schoenberg's expressionistic comic opera, *Von heute auf morgen* (where both the guitar and the mandolin are incorporated in the orchestra), Webern's Two Songs Op. 19, Berg's *Wozzeck* and Boulez's *Marteau sans maître*. Moreover, Rodrigo's popular *Concierto de Aranjuez* vindicated the guitar as an instrument for the modern solo concerto. Modern composers have increasingly turned to the composing of chamber music for the guitar, and not only those of Hispanic countries, among them the Mexican Manuel Ponce or the Brazilian Villa-Lobos, but also such diverse contemporary figures as Davies and Henze (see Henze's *Kammermusik* and *Three Tentos*).

Saxophone The saxophone, named after its inventor Adolphe Sax who patented it in 1846, is a compound instrument created from the fusion of the clarinet and oboe (single reed and conical bore). The body is made of metal in a pipe shape, and all eight in the family are transposing instruments; the most popular are the alto in E♭ and the baritone in E♭. Their notation is written in the treble clef and the normal written compass is from b♭ to f'''. They became immensely popular in brass band ensembles, but above all in jazz bands. In 1939 alone two million were made and sold. It is a remarkably agile instrument with an equally flexible timbre as it possesses both woodwind and brass qualities. Nineteenth-century French composers were quick to adopt the saxophone in their works, of which the most noted example is perhaps Bizet's *L'Arlésienne*. Because of its somewhat dominating timbre, many composers were uncertain about its use in the concert repertory. Nevertheless, a respectable number of twentieth-century composers have also experimented with the saxophone: Debussy in his *Rapsodie* for saxophone and piano and Milhaud in his arrangement of *Scaramouche* for saxophone and piano. Vaughan Williams incorporated it in *Job*, as well as in his Sixth and Ninth Symphonies; it is used in Schoenberg's aforementioned *Von heute auf morgen* and in one of Stockhausen's relatively early works, *Gruppen*.

Harpsichord With the renewed interest in early music the harpsichord had a comeback in twentieth-century compositions not only as a solo and accompanying keyboard instrument, but also as an instrument in its own right. Martinů's Concerto for harpsichord and chamber orchestra, Poulenc's *Concert champêtre*, Falla's Concerto for harpsichord and Carter's Double Concerto are fine examples. An interesting neoclassical revival of the harpsi-

chord accompaniment may be heard in Stravinsky's opera *The Rake's Progress*, based on and inspired by Hogarth's paintings (see Fig. 170).

Fig. 170

Celesta Invented in 1886 by Auguste Mustel in Paris, this instrument looks like a small upright piano with hammer action and all, but the hammers hit metal rods instead of strings, producing an ethereal and mystical sound. Originally it had a four-octave range, but now it is made to cover five octaves, from c upwards. Its notation is like that of the piano (treble and bass), but written an octave lower than the actual sound.

An unforgettable early appearance of the celesta, of course, is to be found in Tchaikovsky's *Nutcracker*, where it evokes the Sugar Plum Fairy. In modern times one of the most striking examples of its use is in the first movement of Bartók's Music for Strings, Percussion and Celesta (see Fig. 75c).

(b) Exotic instruments

Under this heading a selection of instruments has been chosen in order to illustrate the influx of largely Oriental and South American instruments which have enriched the Western musical repertory.

Cimbalom Of Asiatic origin, it established itself in Europe through the Arabs during the Middle Ages. It has been known in Hungary since the fifteenth century, and there became largely associated with folk music, above all with gypsies. Its trapezoid box form now stands on four legs. It has thirty-five courses of metal strings, the upper courses of which have four or five strings to a note. It has two bridges; the strings pass over both or just one or none at all. Its compass is about four octaves, D to e''', and the strings are tuned chromatically. The player strikes the strings with two light sticks which are enlarged and covered at their ends: the 'hammer action' is thus carried out by the player.

During the nineteenth century some Hungarian composers adopted the cimbalom in their orchestras to create a local flavour – Ferenc Erkel in his opera *Bánk bán* and Liszt in his Third Rhapsody for orchestra. During the first quarter of our century

Fig. 171

an extraordinary genius of the cimbalom, Aladar Racz, elevated the instrument into the concert repertory by playing on it his transcriptions of Bach, Couperin and Scarlatti. Saint-Saëns called him the 'Liszt of the Cimbalom'. Racz introduced Stravinsky to the instrument, and the latter eventually used it to good effect in *Renard* and *Rag-time*. Bartók incorporated it in his Rhapsody for violin and Kodály in his *Háry János* (see Fig. 171). More recently, the cimbalom appeared in Boulez's *Eclat* and Davies's *Images, Reflections, Shadows*.

Cowbell Two types of cowbells are played in music, the European and the Latin American. The European cowbell is shaped in the form of the bells worn by cows in central Europe; it has no clapper, and is struck with a stick of the snare drum. Mahler used it in his Sixth Symphony, Richard Strauss in his *Alpensinfonie*. The other type, the cencerro, is similar to the European but of Afro-Arabic origin, and is now largely associated with Cuban light music. Messiaen requires one in *Et exspecto resurrectionem mortuorum*.

Antique cymbals Antique cymbals, or crotales, are two small cymbals either held by leather handles or attached to handles to enable the player to strike them together. The thick metal used by modern makers allows them to tune the cymbals to a definite pitch. The origins of this instrument lie in ancient Egypt, Greece and Rome. Both Debussy and Ravel have written for antique cymbals. The orchestration of Debussy's *Prélude à l'après-midi d'un faune* includes a pair (see p. 172).

Gong There are conflicting opinions concerning the origin of the gong or, as its larger version is known, the tam-tam. Whether it came from South-east Asia and eventually reached Java or directly from China is a matter of debate. What is certain, however, is that it was mentioned in the sixth century in China. These plate-shaped bronze gongs range from two to five feet in diameter and are suspended from a metal frame. The player strikes them in the centre with a stick with a ball-shaped soft end. The sound, usually indefinite, is very penetrating and majestical. Gongs may be heard in Puccini's *Madama Butterfly* and in Holst's 'Mars' from *The Planets*. Messiaen, Stockhausen and Boulez occasionally used them.

Marimba The marimba is really a xylophone with tuned tubular resonators under the wooden plates. These are of different sizes and thicknesses, which are what determine their pitch; the sound can encompass up to seven octaves. The marimba is played with a set of soft-headed mallets, and there can be one or more players, sometimes five. It is of African origin, but established itself in central America, probably through the slave trade, to such an extent that the Guatemalans have made it their national instrument. Paul Creston wrote, as well as a jazz-influenced saxophone concerto, a Concertino for marimba, and Milhaud composed a Concerto for marimba and vibraphone. The marimba is also played in Boulez's *Pli selon pli*, Stockhausen's *Gruppen* and Davies's *Ave maris stella*.

Xylophone The xylophone is similar to the marimba and glock-enspiel, but has a dry tone quality. It is immensely popular in Africa and Java. It covers three or more octaves from middle C upwards. Because of its non-resonant 'woody', almost 'bony' sound, it was chosen by Saint-Saëns in his *Danse macabre* (1874). Since then it has been put to use by several composers, such as Bartók, Messiaen, Stravinsky and Boulez. Particularly fine examples are to be found in Walton's *Belshazzar's Feast* and Schoenberg's *Survivor from Warsaw* (see Fig. 172).

Cow horn The cow horn, an ancient signalling horn, was revived by Wagner in the *Ring* and, more recently, employed by Britten in his *Spring Symphony*.

Fig. 172

(c) New sounds from voices and standard instruments

One of the most striking developments over and above those already touched upon is the way in which the sounds of well-known standard instruments have been explored so that new sounds can be produced. Let us now look at some of these, starting with the most natural of all instruments, the human voice.

Voice *Sprechgesang* has already been discussed (see pp. 159–60), but as it is one of the most markedly expressionistic vocal developments, it is worth repeating its written indication: ♪ . Some composers, among them Ligeti, prefer to use ♪ when the pitch is indefinite

and square notation when the pitch is fixed:

Extremely high *Sprechstimme* is indicated with long stems: ; for very low this is reversed: . Berio, when he requires real

spoken words, uses the following: He also introduced an

indication for breathed utterances:

Ligeti asks the performer to execute *Sprechstimme* while breathing in with the sign . Open mouth is ○ , closed + or ⊟ and half open ⊜ or ⊖ ; ○ can also mean falsetto. Stockhausen calls for hiccup-like sound effects with ▼ . Ligeti indicates a nasal sound with ∿ and a glottal stop with ? . He hit on an ingenious way of indicating the change from voiceless sound to voiced: ⅄ ⟶ ⋁ . Turning the sign round results in the reverse: ⋁ ⟶ ⅄ . Ligeti indicates the spoken word in a score with † ; ▶ means inhale and ◀ exhale. Penderecki introduces laughter in his score with .

Vocalization This technique uses the human voice as if it were an instrument. The singing is wordless or syllabic. Fine examples of this style are Debussy's 'Sirènes' (*Nocturnes* No. 3), Ravel's *Vocalise-étude en forme de habanera*, Delius's *Song of the High Hills* for orchestra and wordless chorus and *A Mass of Life*, Rakhmaninov's 'Vocalise' for voice and piano and Villa–Lobos's *Bachianas brasileiras*.

Strings A characteristic Bartókian sound is the snap pizzicato: or ⌀. These signs are executed by pulling the string so hard that it hits the fingerboard. Another way of playing pizzicato is not in front of but behind the bridge; the sign for this is ↑ . (Kagel on his part prefers φ for snap pizzicato.) Bartók also indicates quarter tones by ↓ and ↑ . Kagel and Penderecki are more specific: Kagel gives ♯ ♭ ♮ for up a quarter, Penderecki ↑♯♭↓ for $(\frac{1}{4})$, $(\frac{3}{4})$ sharpened and flattened quarter notes.

Percussion effect is called for by Bussotti with ○ ; when applied to the violin it tells the player to hit the open strings rhythmically with the left hand. The signs ⊓ and ⊔ are alternatives to the words 'con sordino' and 'senza sordino' (with and without mute).

Penderecki in agreement with Hermann Heiss indicates 'molto vibrato' with ∿∿∿ . For slow vibrato he gives ∿∿ , while Bussotti uses ⟨ . The sign for between bridge and tail piece is ↑. The percussive striking of the body of the stringed instrument with either bow or fingertips is indicated by ♪ or ♩ or ⌐ . The schematized sign ∩ means bow at the bridge.

Among dozens of signs for the harp, the most striking one, forgive the pun, is the request for the strings to be struck with a drumstick: ┼┼┼ or ⊤⟋ .

Percussion The symbols for percussion are as numerous as the instruments, which come from all over the world. On the whole, percussive instruments are marked with signs that look like them. For example:

gong: ⊙

cowbell: ∏

marimba: (M) ▬

xylophone: (X) ▬

antique cymbals: ♁   jingles: ∞

vibraphone: ▱

triangle: △

The symbols for sticks are also easily recognizable, among them:

hard drumstick: ⟋•   triangle rod: ⧖

soft drumstick: ⟋°   wooden mallet ⟍◾

glockenspiel hammer: ⟋⌐

Problems arise, however, with performance symbols, as these are much less obvious. Kagel gives ⚭ for drop stick on skin, ⦿ for keeping the stick depressed and φ for rimshot (hitting the rim of the drum). Friedrich Cerha's sign for rimshot is ✕. Stockhausen calls for the crashing of cymbals with ⊣⊢. For irregular tremolo Penderecki uses this picturesque sign: ⨲ . There can be little doubt that the signs for each score must be studied carefully so that the highly personal indications of each composer can be mastered.

Traditional indications at least aimed towards universality, but the modern tendency is to adopt a variety of notational styles and to cultivate individual idiosyncrasies in notation, symbols of performance and the like.

Wind instruments The repeating of notes by quick movements of the tongue in twos or threes is indicated by ⌐···⌐ ⌐···⌐ ; to blow without tone is ⧧ . The following curious sign calls for the hitting of the mouthpiece with the palm of the hand: ⊤ ⊤ . Glissando effects, up and down, are ⟋ ⟍ . To make a vocal sound at the given pitch while playing the instrument is indicated by: 𝄞

Keyboard instruments A silent cluster (depressing several notes at one time) is:  . The following indicate a cluster on white keys only and black keys only respectively:

Chromatic clusters to be played with the arms are usually marked with a thick black line covering the whole compass of the requested notes, whether they fall in the bass or treble clef or across both: █

For harmonics on the piano the indication is: . The lower note is played, but the upper is silently depressed. Stockhausen gives this tadpole sign for rapid repetition of one note:

The use of the inside of the piano for new sound effects has also contributed to the increase in signs. Here are some examples:

(a) strike strings with hand:

(b) scrape bass strings with a metal plate: ⋁⋀⋁⋀⋀⋀⋀⋀⋀⋀⋀⋀⋀⋀⋁

(c) pluck strings with fingernail:

(d) pluck string with finger: ⋃

(e) strike piano lid against framework: ▭•

(f) glissando inside over strings or glissando with finger: ∪⌒

It should be noted that all these signs represent only a fraction of those currently used, which are as numerous as composers and compositions. The aim here has been to introduce the reader to some of them, and to draw attention to the wide variety of sound effects which have been mushrooming during this century. For further detailed references and studies, the reader is referred to the Bibliography.

(d) Musical use of extra-musical sound-making sources

We know that for realistic sound effects Tchaikovsky used guns for his *1812* overture. It would be easy to find striking examples of unusual sound effects in the works of composers from the Middle Ages to the end of the nineteenth century. The ancestry is distinguished. The idea of emancipating not only dissonance but noise as well, however (the two are not necessarily the same), is a characteristically twentieth-century phenomenon. Schoenberg asks for big iron chains in his *Gurrelieder*. The most famously entertaining example to this day is the use of extra-musical sound-making sources in Satie's *Parade*. In it he includes pistol shots, a rattle, a roulette wheel, sirens, a typewriter (which turns out to be a remarkably effective percussion instrument) and water splashes, to say nothing of the circus music and the bruitist (see p. 288) and neoclassical musical *tour de force* played by the rest of the orchestra. An equally fascinating composition in which noise-making elements are combined with unusual instruments is George Antheil's *Ballet mécanique*, whose title speaks for itself. In it he calls for the sound effects of both large and small aeroplane propellers.

To all the above types of sound effects should be added those of the spoken voice. The reading of dramatic or poetic texts, shouts, whispers, sneers, laughter, syllabic, quasi-instrumental vocalization and so on can be incorporated into a composition for evocative, psycho-dramatic reasons. There are plenty of good examples in the repertory, from Debussy's 'Sirènes' to Davies's *Eight Songs for a Mad King* and Birtwistle's *Punch and Judy*. Perhaps one of the most poetic instances is the third movement of Berio's *Sinfonia*.

(e) New instruments

The futurist movement, which was at its peak between the years 1909 and 1919, had a major role to play in the visual arts and literature. Its participants backed it with numerous manifestos and revolutionary pamphlets in which they projected their vision of the new men and new art in an age of science and technology. The movement had, of course, an impact on fellow artists, as well as on practitioners in music. Among musicians, some were aggressively projecting modernism and futurism at all costs, with an almost total rejection of the past. Francesco Balilla Pratella, one of the first futurist musicians, was writing manifestos concerning futurist music as early as 1910–12; in these he welcomed the use of atonality, quarter tones and asymmetric rhythms and the legitimate application of noise. Futurism is discussed further in Chapter Six. What interests us here is the futurists' involvement with strange sound effects, including noise, and their attempts at making noise machines. In a sense the futurists were playing with musical ideas which were fully realized only after the Second World War with the emergence of *musique concrète* and electronic music.

Intonarumori This is the Italian for noise-makers. It was used by Luigi Russolo to denote a group of instruments invented by him on which, supposedly, it was possible to make mechanical sounds and rhythmic patterns. These were largely manipulated mechanically or sometimes in combination with electricity. Russolo gave several fanciful names to his machines, such as scoppiatone (exploder) and ululatore (yelling machine), all in the spirit of futurist onomatopoeia. Unfortunately, we have but the vaguest idea of how these instruments sounded, as they were destroyed during the Second World War, but contemporary photographs show a cubist–futurist visual display of loudspeakers and noise-making boxes manipulated by musicians.

Vibraphone This new instrument is based on a similar principle to that of the marimba. It is made of metal and has electrically generated propellers under each metal bar which make the sound vibrate; its compass is f–f'''. Lionel Hampton, a jazz player, was the instrument's first great performer. It is used mainly in dance bands, but quickly found its place in the modern repertory: Berg's *Lulu*, Messiaen's *Trois petites liturgies*, Milhaud's Concerto for marimba and vibraphone and Stockhausen's *Refrain*. Several others have written for it, including Vaughan Williams.

Theremin and ondes martenot The bruitists (the musical section of the futurist movement) were interested not only in noise, but also in mechanically or electronically manipulated sound-makers. Independently, though, and in a kindred spirit, two inventors, the Franco-Russian physicist Léon Thérémin and the Frenchman Maurice Martenot, developed electronically controlled melody instruments in the 1920s which can be viewed as the forerunners of electronic music. These developments made a profound impression on the musical thinking of Cowell and, above all, Varèse.

The tone in the theremin is produced by two high-frequency circuits and two oscillating valves, of which one is constant and the other is altered by the proximity of the player's hand. It plays only one note at a time within a range of five octaves. It can produce sounds similar to the human voice, but also several instrumental effects. The sound is amplified by a loudspeaker. Although employed by some composers – notably Martinů, who wrote a Fantasie for theremin, string quartet, oboe and piano – it never really caught on, and remained a passing, if fascinating, experiment.

In collaboration with Thérémin, Cowell developed an instrument capable of the most complex rhythmic effects, called the rhythmicon. This too, however, did not become established.

Martenot's invention, the ondes martenot (martenot waves) or ondes musicales (musical waves), is not unlike the theremin in that it also works on the principle of the action between a fixed and a variable oscillation and the proximity of the player's hand to a receiver (a stretched cord or cords). But whereas the theremin is rather primitive in construction, the ondes martenot is performed on a keyboard of seven octaves. It can play only one note at a time, but it can control timbre and volume, and glissando effects can be produced. Because of its greater versatility, it became quite popular, particularly among French composers. It may be heard in, for example, Varèse's *Ecuatorial*, Milhaud's Suite with piano, Messiaen's *Turangalîla-symphonie* and Honegger's *Jeanne d'Arc au bûcher*.

The expansion of percussion instruments The emphatic preoccupation with rhythm during this century, combined with the emancipation of both dissonance and noise, brought about an unprecedented interest in percussion instruments and their increased use in various types of compositions as well as scoring for percussion alone, as in Varèse's *Ionisation*. The collective term 'percussion' represents a vast number of instruments from all over the world which have in common their method of producing sound through some form of striking action. This may be generated by fingers, hands, sticks or a striking mechanism, such as the hammer action of the piano. It is for this reason that during our century the piano has been treated as a percussive instrument by Stravinsky, Bartók, Cage, Varèse, Stockhausen and numerous other leading composers.

Percussion instruments fall into two main categories, those with definite pitch (for example timpani) and those without definite pitch (for example cymbals). Those with definite pitch are perhaps in greater demand than those without, but what is remarkable is the vast proliferation of percussion instruments in Western music. One of the main causes of this is likely to be our greater awareness of and contact and involvement with non-European musical cultures. Western music is no longer seen as the focal point of musical expression and music-making, and nor is there a romantic view of musical universality coming from the West. Instead music is practised with a much more realistic and pragmatic absorption of the universality of sound through the synthesis of, for instance, African, Indian, Chinese, Javanese and Indonesian musical cultures.

The prepared piano In the 1930s and 1940s Cage, who made a special point of cultivating rhythm and percussion music, wrote for percussion ensembles, and also organized and performed in them. The Californian-born Cowell, who was Ives's friend and biographer, and one of the great American pioneers of music, hit on the idea of the prepared piano, that is, not only playing with the inside of the piano, but also altering its sound by placing on or inserting in the strings various kinds of metal or wooden objects, such as coins, drawing-pins, nails and screws. He too was involved with percussion music, as his late work Concerto for Percussion demonstrates. Cage was very much influenced by Cowell, and he followed up and further developed the prepared piano, for which he became one of the most inventive writers. A fascinating aural experience for those not familiar with the style is to hear *A Room* played on a normal piano and then on a prepared piano. The first version has a Bartókian quality to it, reminiscent of his 'From the Diary of a Fly' (*Mikrokosmos* Vol. VI No. 142). Cage's piece is dominated by ostinato and percussive effects (see Fig. 173), which

Fig. 173 ©1968 by Henmar Press Inc., New York. Reproduced by permission of Peters Edition Ltd, London

are further emphasized when the piece is played on the prepared piano. This version sounds like Indonesian gamelan music; as the piano is prepared, the various timbres give an illusion of a percussive ensemble, though there is only one player. The visit paid by the Javanese gamelan musicians to the World Fair in Paris in 1889, which made such a deep impression on Debussy and Ravel, to this day carries on exercising a profound influence on the thinking of many composers.

Partch's instruments Like Cowell, Harry Partch was a Californian and a rebellious pioneer. He rejected the even-tempered Western system and replaced it with a microtonal system which has, in place of the twelve semitones in an octave, forty-three microtones. In this he followed Oriental practice and theories. Moreover, his music was physical and theatre-oriented, rather in the manner of classical Greek drama and Japanese Noh plays, where acting, dancing, singing, staging and instrumental music-making are all combined for a quasi-ritualistic experience. Partch shared with some of his contemporary musicians a dissatisfaction with the constraining effect of conventional instruments, on which his microtonal ideas could not easily be played. His dissatisfaction turned him into an inventor and maker of new, mainly percussive instruments, which he based largely on Polynesian examples. These new instruments are visually very decorative; the sound of, for instance, his gourd tree and cone gongs resembles Oriental percussive instruments. He also extended the marimba family with his own inventions (such as bass marimba, marimba eroica) and made a reed organ with a keyboard, called the chromelodeon, on which the forty-three microtones per octave are playable. Unfortunately, after his death in 1976 both his instruments and his music turned into generally inaccessible curiosity items wrapped up in the care of the Harry Partch Foundation of San Diego, California.

Klangfarbenmelodie

The history of orchestration shows a gradual unfolding of colouristic possibilities from the time of Monteverdi to our century. From Berlioz onwards the preoccupation with orchestral timbre in its own right gained increased attention and importance, until Schoenberg, in the third of his Five Orchestral Pieces Op. 16, put into practice the ultimate concept of treating this timbre as an equal in structural terms to pitch, duration, rhythm and so on. In his book *Harmonielehre* (published in 1911) he put forward the idea of composing 'colour melody' or 'timbre melody' by changing tone colours even if the pitch remains on a single note. Although it was Schoenberg who had initiated the idea of *Klangfarbenmelodie*, it was his pupil, Webern, who adopted it to the point of obsession, making it a personal trade mark of his composition. A fascinating introduction to the use of *Klangfarbenmelodie* is Webern's orchestration of Bach's Ricercar from the *Musical Offering*. The two illustrations given here come from one of his own works, Five Pieces for orchestra Op. 10. Fig. 174a shows the *Klangfarbenmelodie* applied to varying pitch, while Fig. 174b illustrates its application when the pitch is at the same level.

Fig. 174a ∧ **Fig. 174b** ∨

The disintegration of seating arrangements

The seating arrangements for chamber music have changed little, though some chamber-sized compositions, such as Bartók's Sonata for two pianos and percussion, call for arrangements which allow the performers to see each other. It should be remembered that what matters when planning seating, be it for chamber or orchestral music, are the acoustic considerations and the blending and dovetailing of the instruments to create the most effective sound and to facilitate collaboration and contact between players.

The seating plans of the orchestra have been drastically modified, reflecting the many changes it has undergone during this century. A classical or romantic symphonic orchestra had a basic set plan to which the listener became accustomed (see Fig. 175). An individual conductor might prefer to separate the first violins from the second violins by placing one to his left and the other to his right, or to rearrange the wind instruments by having all the woodwind in a single line and the brass players in another, but the diversion from the overall traditional plan would be minimal. In the twentieth century the inclusion of many new instruments, whether Western or Oriental, changed the familiar classical plan, as did the possible exclusion of standard members of the orchestra and the new combinations of forces which ranged from chamber size to monumental, from a single to multiple orchestras. Anything can and does happen, as may be observed in such works as Schoenberg's First Chamber Symphony, Xenakis's *Terretektorh*, where players place themselves among the audience, Stockhausen's *Gruppen* and Carter's Symphony of Three Orchestras, which calls for multiple orchestras.

To gain better control some composers thought to form their own orchestras, among them Cage and the minimalist Philip Glass. Other groups were established in order to specialize in contemporary music, for example the Contemporary Chamber Ensemble, the London Sinfonietta and Fires of London. It should be noted, however, that these are all small ensembles; the costs of running a large orchestra are enormous.

Musique concrète

In 1948 the French composr Pierre Schaeffer introduced a 'Concert of Noises' on French radio. The futurists' dream was vindicated by a renewed wave of interest in legitimizing noise and by electronic manipulation of sound. Schaeffer's intention was unambiguous: 'I decided to choose my musical elements in the contrary domain from that of music, in noises.' The compositional style which he evolved became known as *musique concrète*, or concrete music. The principal ideas behind it are:

(a) The traditional interpretation of music is discarded for that of noise.
(b) Any sound is fit for composition.
(c) The music is prepared from recorded sounds. These may be selected from nature or artificial sound effects (a barking dog, birdsong, a waterfall, thunder, traffic, factory noise, an aeroplane, manipulated instruments and so on), as well as vocal sound effects (such as speaking, crying and shouting).
(d) Tape is manipulated (for example tapes are combined in montage, speeded up, slowed down, played backwards, timbre is modified by filters and modulators).

The following selected list of compositions will serve as a sound introduction to the world of *musique concrète*: Pierre Schaeffer's *Symphonie pour un homme seul*, Pierre Henry's *Le Voile d'Orphée*, Messiaen's *Timbres-durées*, Varèse's *Poème électronique* and Stockhausen's *Gesang der Jünglinge*. Initially the aim of those practising *musique concrète* proper was distinct from that of the slowly evolving 'pure' electronic music-makers, but in time the differences became considerably blurred, largely because the two styles were mixed by some composers, including Varèse and Stockhausen.

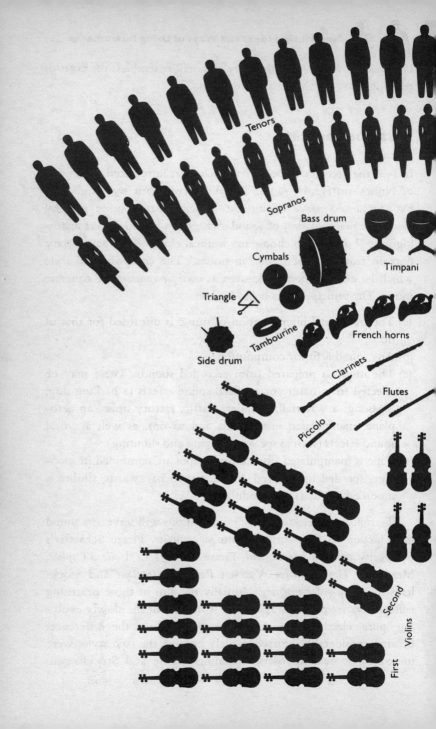

Tenors

Sopranos

Cymbals

Bass drum

Triangle

Timpani

Tambourine

French horns

Side drum

Clarinets

Flutes

Piccolo

Second

Violins

First

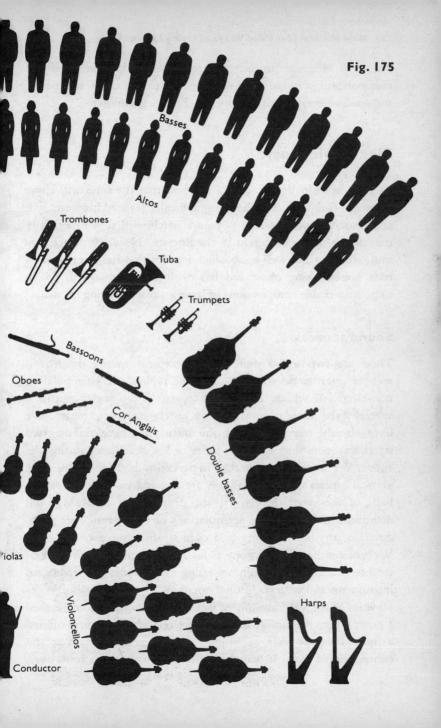

Fig. 175

Basses

Altos

Trombones

Tuba

Trumpets

Bassoons

Oboes

Cor Anglais

Double basses

Violas

Violoncellos

Harps

Conductor

The term 'electronic music' now refers to anything in which the manipulation of sound is primarily generated by electronic means, and *musique concrète* is used only in its historical context.

Electronic music

As early as 1936 Varèse said, 'I am sure that the time will come when the composer, after he has graphically realized his score, will see this score automatically put on a machine that will faithfully transmit the musical content to the listener.' Nowadays electronic music-making is a well-established activity that has outgrown its rude noise-making phase and has evolved a language in which some remarkable compositions of lasting value are being created.

Sound sources

There are two sound sources for electronic music: the first is *musique concrète*, based on the idea of taping and manipulating non-electronic sounds; the second represents the purist approach, whereby the sound is produced by purely electronic means. We have already mentioned that the distinction between the two styles was soon blurred; it was more or less abandoned during the 1960s. We have also seen that in serialism both the linear and vertical aspects of a composition are derived from the common basis of the series. Moreover, the principle of serialism could determine all the possible permutations of each parameter: pitch, duration, rhythm, intensity and even timbre. Some of the post-Webern composers have gone as far as is possible with the idea of total serialization while still expressing musical ideas on traditional instruments and with traditional notation. The mathematical complexities of the working-out of some of the compositions reached a point where the rapidly developing electronic inventions offered a more adequate technical solution to the realization of certain compositional ideas. It was then that electronic music took over, as it were, and it thus represents a logical continuation of Webern's obsessive preoccupation with serialism as an absolute dominating force in compositional thinking.

The term 'electronic music' has been applied to two approaches: *musique concrète* and the 'purist' or 'absolute' electronic styles. It therefore embraces two distinct styles of electronic sound manipulation, that is, the use of tapes, and the synthesizer as well as the computer. Since the term 'computer music', however, seems to have distanced itself from the general umbrella of electronic music, it is more often than not used in its specific sense. (This is discussed on pp. 223-4.)

Tape studios

Tape studios have been in operation since the late 1940s and early 1950s. These studios were equipped with sound generators and sound modifying and mixing equipment, together with, of course, recording facilities. The two schools of thought in electronic music-making were operating in the studios of France under Schaeffer and of Germany largely under Herbert Eimert and Stockhausen. These were shortly followed by the establishment of a studio at Radio Italiano in Milan, where electronic music was composed by Berio and Maderna. Since the 1950s studios have been proliferating in both America and Europe, especially on university campuses.

Pure electronic music

In order to produce characteristic electronically made sound effects, such as sine-tones, square waves, white noise and other complex combinations, signal and noise generators are employed.

Sine-tone A sine-tone is a pure tone, that is, a tone without overtones.

Square wave A square wave is the opposite of a sine-tone as it contains a rich selection of odd-numbered partials (overtones).

White noise White noise, or white sound, is the result of a random distribution of all frequencies sounding simultaneously. As it contains all the frequencies within the range of the generator's response curve, there is no period of oscillation; instead of a wave, a straight line representing the summation of infinite numbers of frequencies is produced.

All the technical tricks involving manipulation of tapes as outlined in connection with *musique concrète* are equally applicable to pure electronic music: montage, speeding up, slowing down, modifying timbre and so on. Filters and ring modulators came into increased prominence in electronic music-making.

Filter A filter is an electronic device which enables manipulation of the frequencies in a sound.

Ring modulator From the fusion of two signals a ring modulator can produce two new tones based on the sum of their combination and of their difference. For instance, if a sine-tone is 250 cps (cycles per second) and another is 350 cps, one tone will be 250 + 350 = 600 cps and the other will be the difference: 350 − 250 = 100 cps.

Synthesizer It was Robert Moog who invented voltage-controlled oscillators and amplifiers, which led him, in the 1960s, to the assembling of the synthesizer. This machine turned out to be one of the most versatile instruments, for it is capable of playing very complicated musical structures and sound combinations without needing recording and tape editing. Composers were thus in total control of immediate sound effects, which they could freely manipulate as they wished. In a way, a synthesizer could be seen as an extension of a studio, but it has the advantage over the traditional studio of being able to combine sequencing and voltage control, which considerably increases the possibilities of sound manipulations. Perhaps the most important benefit of a synthesizer is that it enables the composer to hear these sounds instantly. This composition and its immediate live realization give an electronic composer working on a synthesizer a practical advantage over not only a traditional composer, but also the *musique concrète* and early studio composers.

Nonesuch Records and Turnabout Records have issued some fine electronic compositions. An interesting example is Andrew Rudin's *Tragoedia*, whose sound sources include white noise, sine-tones and a single burst of sound called a pulse. It contains four movements, of 10, 7.5, 5 and 15 minutes' duration. Similarly fascinating are Babbitt's Composition for Synthesizer and Ensembles for Synthesizer. These serve as a good introduction to pure electronic music.

Computer music

Computer music is based on the acoustic fact that any sound has numerically translatable properties, such as pitch, timbre and amplitude. These numerical codes of sounds, when fed into a computer, can be 'realized' (that is, made audible) when the computer output is fed into a digital-to-analogue converter. This electric instrument can transform the numerical product of a digital computer into a magnetic tape for a real sound play-back. All this was, until the 1980s, a very slow, complicated and labour-intensive method which did not allow the composer to hear the work until the whole process of numerical calculation and digital-to-analogue converting was completed. But in the 1990s, with the rapid evolution of technical developments such as the compact disc and the NICAM 728 (Near Instantaneously Compounded Audio Multiplex; 728 indicates a digital byte-rate of 728,000 bytes per second), slow realization belongs to the past. Computer music makes use of the incredible power and speed of the modern digital microcomputer to achieve this processing almost instantly. The sound must first be converted into machine-readable form by sampling it at very high frequency in an analogue-to-digital converter (ADC) which generates digital codes for the computer. When the composer wishes to hear the effect(s) of his or her work, the digital output from the computer is reconverted to analogue form by passing it through a digital-to-analogue converter (DAC) to drive the sound-producing system. Ten years in computing science, from 1980 to 1990, is a very long time, and there have been incredible developments in technical sophistication. This style of electronic music is perhaps best represented by Vladimir Ussachevsky's Computer Piece No. 1 and Two Sketches for a Computer Piece. There are now classics in a growing repertory.

Performing electronic music

Since with electronic music composing and performing are not separate activities that require a concert hall, the whole concept of traditional concert performance has been challenged. Once the electronic composition is ready, what is needed is a record or cassette player to replay the product. This can be done anywhere and at any time. The potential for depersonalization and audience alienation inherent in electronic music led some composers to mix live performance and electronic music, or to give live electronic ensemble performances in such a way that the concert occasion is retained. Several of Stockhausen's pieces belong to this genre, for instance *Mantra* (for two pianos and electronics), *Mikrophonie I* (for tam-tam and electronics), *Mikrophonie II* (for chorus, Hammond organ and electronics) and *Prozession* (live electronic ensemble). Stockhausen himself toured with his live electronic ensemble; other ensembles were formed, including the Musica Elettronica Viva, which won acclaim during the second half of the 1960s and early 1970s. Since then live performances of electronic music, with the paraphernalia of electronic equipment, cables and all, have become an established part of the concert repertory.

Stockhausen became increasingly engulfed in his own music to the exclusion of all others. Moreover, he has envisaged the erection of a special building, not unlike Wagner's Bayreuth, entirely dedicated to the performance of his own music; it has grown to Wagnerian proportions.

In the mid-1970s Boulez, with an equally egocentric attitude, founded and became the director of the Institut de Recherche et de Coordination Acoustique/Musique in Paris, where advanced experimental music-making is still taking place. In Europe this is one of the most prestigious centres for electronic and computer composition and research.

There can be no doubt that electronic music has created for itself a most useful place in producing sound effects in film, television, radio and the pop music industry (see, for example, the Beatles' album *Sgt Pepper's Lonely Hearts Club Band*). In the concert repertory such works as Varèse's *Poème électronique*, Stockhausen's *Gesang der Jünglinge* and *Mantra*, Gerhard's Symphony No. 3 'Collages' and Babbitt's Ensembles for Synthesizer are already established works. Since 1945–6 the world of electronics has evolved with astonishing speed. Improvements in terms of technical sophistication take place each year. It is likely that in the future, when the fervour of experimentation will have settled down, the time will come for the creation of works which will be characterized not so much by the experimenting and pioneering spirit as by mature consolidation and the full artistic use of the available vast sound materials. The Brahms of electronic music is yet to come, but, whether we like it or not, electronic music is here to stay.

CHAPTER FIVE

The Amalgamation of Diverse Musical
Sources: *the past, Mediterranean influence, folk music, the influence of popular music, non-Western exotic effects*

The closest Western civilization has come to unity since the Congress of Vienna in 1815 was the week that the *Sgt Pepper* album was released.

LANGDON WINNER

During its long history Western European music has absorbed a considerable amount of musical influences via its encounters, largely through trading and wars, with non-Western European countries and civilizations. It is, for example, well documented that most of our musical instruments originated in Asia and were adopted in the Middle Ages. These encounters with other civilizations often left their marks in the form of stylistic vogues for 'things foreign' which, from time to time, swept across Europe. European architecture, interior decoration and porcelain show very clearly the fashionable phases of interest in Arabic, Turkish, Chinese and Japanese styles. In music a well-known example of one of these fashions is the so-called Turkish phase which for a time exercised a superficial influence on the music of both Mozart and Beethoven. During the twentieth century, however, largely boosted by electronic communication and travelling facilities, an unparalleled cross-fertilization has been and is taking place to such an extent that to use the word 'universal' cannot be an exaggeration. A characteristic aspect of twentieth-century music is its coalescent, synthesizing nature. This chapter will examine some of the influences which have had a striking impact on

Western musical thinking. For the sake of convenience these have been grouped into five categories: the past; the Mediterranean; folk music; popular music; and non-Western exotic effects.

The past: medieval, Renaissance, baroque and classical influences

Until well into the nineteenth century the idea of a composer turning to the past in order to evoke an earlier style, albeit in an original way, was unheard of. By and large music was an art of the present. But with the growth of research activities and the rapid popularization of the results through publications, performances and musical societies promoting ancient music, the new awareness of the past brought a change in our musical perception and in our relation to contemporary music. To what extent musical historicism added to the alienation of the audience from contemporary composers is a matter for debate, but it can hardly be overlooked. One should remember that although the Archbishop of Salzburg did not like Mozart's music, his preference was for the contemporary Italian style, not for the past, while today many music lovers seem to reject twentieth-century music in favour of the music of bygone ages. This is a relatively new phenomenon. For centuries the teaching of music was based largely on the study of contemporary practices. Bach's method, for instance, was to examine the music of masters of his time. It was during the nineteenth century that the focus on old masters, to the virtual exclusion of the contemporary musical scene, came about. To this day this is the dominating method of teaching, though there have been some encouraging efforts to bring about a better-balanced curriculum.

Medieval and Renaissance influence

During this century several composers have turned to the past to evoke it and, as we have seen in previous chapters, to enrich their musical languages. Debussy's use of the medieval parallel organum technique, based on the idea of melodic harmonization by adding one, two or more parts mostly in parallel motion, is apparent in several of his compositions. A most notable example is 'La Cathédrale engloutie' (*Préludes* Bk 1; see Fig. 43).

Other composers who have succeeded in evoking the medieval style in a modern disguise are Orff, in his popular *Carmina burana*, Stravinsky, in his Cantata, and Davies. Davies's borrowing and modern paraphrasing have become characteristic features of his compositional style; old ideas and materials are metamorphosed, often out of recognition, into a world of serialism and deliberate distortions, sometimes leading to parody. The interaction of the post-Webern and post-modernist approach and the medieval and Renaissance elements in his music achieves a convincing cohesion. Such works as the *Alma Redemptoris mater*, which is based on a motet of Dunstable, O *magnum mysterium* (see Fig. 176), a didactic masterpiece, or *Missa super l'homme armé* illustrate this interaction.

With the dawn of the second British musical renaissance one is confronted with a vigorous revivalist tendency in matters of musicology and of the performance of old English music. Most important of all is the deliberate linking up with a glorious musical past after the lean years which befell music in England between Purcell and Elgar. It is perhaps not by accident that Vaughan Williams's noble Fantasia on a Theme by Thomas Tallis for double string orchestra and string quartet honoured a great native Renaissance master while inaugurating the emergence of a new era of British music in 1910. It evoked an antiphonal modal world which, while being a tribute to the past, introduced an authentically modern English style.

Peter Warlock was another British musician influenced by the past. His musicological interest led him to write about Elizabethan

Fig. 176

and Jacobean English ayres, as well as a fascinating book in collaboration with Cecil Gray on a Renaissance madrigalist, *Carlo Gesualdo: Musician and Murderer*. As a composer Warlock left a fine homage in his *Capriol Suite*, consisting of six arrangements of old dances from Arbeau's famous late medieval and Renaissance dance collection, *Orchésographie*.

There are many twentieth-century composers in whose works medieval and Renaissance elements, above all modal thinking, are apparent, among them such fine composition of Hugo Distler as *Totentanz*. Brief or sustained modal writing may be found in the compositions listed below. The Ionian mode, being the equivalent of our C major scale, is omitted; we start therefore on D, the Dorian mode.

Dorian mode
Debussy: *Pelléas et Mélisande*
Ravel: String Quartet in F major
Respighi: *Concerto gregoriano*

Phrygian mode
Debussy: String Quartet in G minor
Bartók: *Mikrokosmos* Vol. I No. 34
Shostakovich: Symphony No. 5

Lydian mode
Sibelius: Symphony No. 4
Ravel: *Trois chansons*
Britten: Seven Sonnets of Michelangelo

Mixolydian mode
Satie: *Gymnopédie* No. 2
Bartók: Piano Concerto No. 3
Britten: Serenade Op. 31

Aeolian mode
Orff: *Carmina burana*
Respighi: *Pines of Rome*
Walton: *Façade*

Locrian mode
Debussy: Sonata for flute, viola and harp
Hindemith: *Ludus tonalis*
Sibelius: Symphony No. 4

Mixed modality
Bartók: String Quartet No. 3
Debussy: *Le Martyre de St Sébastien*
Poulenc: *Mouvements perpétuels* No. 2
Ravel: Piano Concerto in G major

Pre-classical influence

In Chapter Three, on musical forms and textures, we saw that the renewed interest in pre-classical music, the 'Back to Bach' movement, gave new life to several typically baroque musical procedures, the concerto grosso, suite, fugue, oratorio, cantata and so forth. Composers such as Busoni, Stravinsky, Bartók, members of Les Six and Hindemith made conscious efforts to amalgamate these elements into their musical thinking in a highly original manner. One of the main reasons why this return to earlier musical styles and search for musical ancestry came about was that modern composers, especially during the earlier part of the twentieth century, felt the need to get away from nineteenth-century romanticism, which was seen as being characterized by subjective emotionalism. In pre-romantic music they believed that they had found an enriching ancestral link between past and present. The inherent danger in composing modern works influenced by old styles is the possibility of turning out mannerist pastiches. In the hands of the masters, however, a real musical metamorphosis took place, as is surely the case with the second movement of Stravinsky's Symphony of Psalms. His famous *Pulcinella* ballet and the suite based on the works by Pergolesi, charming as they are, are nearer to pastiche, but in such works as his *Ebony Concerto* the baroque elements are transfigured into the twentieth-century idiom. Another interesting feature of Stravinsky's and Bartók's

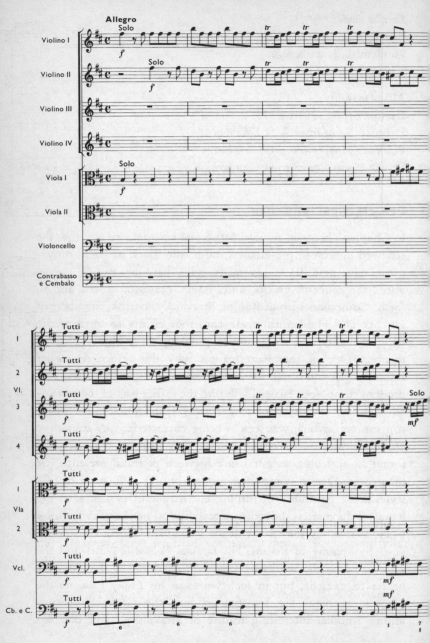

< **Fig. 177a   Fig. 177b** ∧

revival of the baroque in our century is their use of ostinato rhythm, which is not unlike the baroque concerto style. The influence of folk music on both composers should also be taken into account. The two examples in Fig. 177, from Vivaldi's Concerto in B minor Op. 3 No. 10 and Bartók's *Divertimento*, illustrate that the repetitive, quasi-motoric ostinato rhythms have a striking similarity. In the case of Stravinsky the ostinato technique became a personal musical insignia, especially of his so-called neoclassical period.

What epitomizes an elegant absorption of pre-classical musical style into twentieth-century thinking is Ravel's refined preoccupation with the past as revealed in several of his compositions, for example the well-known *Pavane pour une infante défunte* and, above all, *Le Tombeau de Couperin*, a suite for piano composed in 1917 and later orchestrated by the composer. It consists of six movements (Prelude, Fugue, Forlane, Rigaudon, Menuet and Toccata, all characteristically pre-classical), each dedicated to one of his friends who died during the First World War. Through this gesture Ravel pays homage not only to his lost friends and, of course, to Couperin, but also, as if by magic, to the French classical past and values inherent in French civilization.

Classical influences

It is most revealing that the basic call of the French group Les Six (Auric, Durey, Honegger, Milhaud, Poulenc and Tailleferre), under the influence of Satie and Cocteau, was for a return to French classicism and, more importantly, a turning against romanticism. This encompassed Schoenberg, in whom they saw the apotheosis of German romanticism. They stated their desire for classical transparency and economy. 'Back to diatonic music' and 'abandon chromaticism' was the creed of the day, chromaticism being one of the most characteristic features of the romantic musical language which they set out to avoid. Accordingly, the music of Couperin, Rameau, Haydn and Mozart was studied for its clarity and grace. Debussy's first set for solo piano under the title *Images*, composed as early as 1905, contains a 'Hommage à Rameau'. It was with a *jeu d'esprit* that Prokofiev's symphonic *tour de force* the Classical Symphony, written in the style of 'Papa' Haydn, came about. It is structured in the classical symphonic four-movement plan. For the third movement, however, Prokofiev replaced the traditional

minuet with a gavotte, a French dance in 4/4 time which begins
on the third beat of the bar. Like the minuet, the gavotte became
popular during the reign of Louis XIV, the Sun King, and was an
optional movement of the baroque suite. That is why it was
included in Schoenberg's Suite for string orchestra. The main
themes from Prokofiev's Classical Symphony illustrate the diatonic
nature of the melodies, while the first page of the full score
demonstrates the transparent, classical scoring (see Figs. 99, 178).

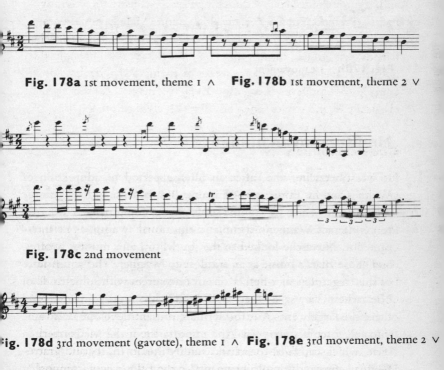

Fig. 178a 1st movement, theme 1 ∧   **Fig. 178b** 1st movement, theme 2 ∨

Fig. 178c 2nd movement

Fig. 178d 3rd movement (gavotte), theme 1 ∧   **Fig. 178e** 3rd movement, theme 2 ∨

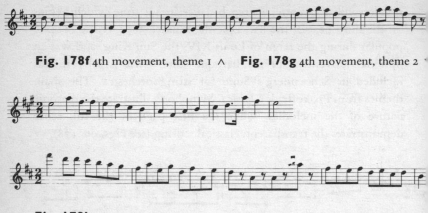

Fig. 178f 4th movement, theme 1 ∧   **Fig. 178g** 4th movement, theme 2

Fig. 178h　1st movement

Mediterranean influence

It was Nietzsche who, after an intense period of admiration of Wagner and his music, turned against him because of his Teutonic grandeur, in which he saw the seeds of a looming danger. In order to counteract Wagner's chromatic emotional swamp, as he interpreted it, Nietzsche looked to the south, to Latin musical sources, and chose Bizet's music as an antidote to Wagner. The significance of this, regardless of whether or not one agrees with some or all of Nietzsche's views, is that well before the anti-romantic, and therefore largely anti-Austro-German, musical developments came into full force he recognized the importance of the Mediterranean style, which had been overshadowed by the north, that is, Austro-German music, during the romantic period. One could argue that Bizet's incidental music to *L'Arlésienne* shows him to be nearer in spirit to Les Six, above all Milhaud and Poulenc, than any other composers of the time, apart from Chabrier. An interesting exercise is to listen to Bizet's *L'Arlésienne* suites, then Chabrier's *Joyeuse marche*, followed by Milhaud's *Suite provençale* or *Suite française*. The experience is most revealing, as well as uplifting: the listener acquires a musical 'suntan'.

From the last quarter of the nineteenth century onwards the Mediterranean world – particularly Spain, whose heavy scents and sensuous blend of Arabic and Christian influences gain expression in ritualistic encounters such as fiestas, with colourful songs and dances, and the bull fight, itself a kind of *danse macabre* – has stimulated the imagination of several composers. The list is impressive. Here is a selection of compositions written by both native and foreign composers to prove the case, starting, of course, with Bizet's *Carmen*, a work Nietzsche greatly admired.

Bizet: *Carmen*
Rimsky-Korsakov: *Spanish Caprice*
Chabrier: *España*
Albéniz: *Suite Iberia, Rapsodia española*
Debussy: *Ibéria, Six épigraphes antiques*
Ravel: *Rapsodie espagnole, Alborada del gracioso, L'Heure espagnole,*
    Don Quichotte à Dulcinée, Boléro
Ibert: *Le Chevalier errant, Escales*
Falla: *La vida breve, El amor brujo, Noches en los jardines de España,*
    El sombrero de tres picos, Siete canciones populares españolas
Massenet: *Don Quichotte*
R. Strauss: *Don Quixote*
Petrassi: *Ritratto di Don Chisciotte*
Gerhard: *Don Quixote*

Other references to the Mediterranean include Satie's *Gymnopédies*, Ravel's *Daphnis et Chloé* and *Cinq mélodies populaires grecques* and Respighi's symphonic poems *Fountains of Rome, Pines of Rome* and *Roman Festival*.

Apart from Strauss's *Don Quixote*, which notably fails to do so, all these works, in one way or another, succeeded in evoking the spirit of the Mediterranean world in sound with vivid colours and rhythm, a world which is so distinct from the northern and central European temperament and Teutonic musical tradition.

Herein lies the liberating influence it exercised from around the turn of this century. In order to illustrate at least one aspect of the style Fig. 179 provides a fine example from Debussy's *Ibéria*, of which Falla said that it was not written in the Spanish *manner*, but *in* Spanish. It comes from its third movement, entitled 'Le Matin d'un jour de fête'. 'It sounds like music which has not been written down!' declared Debussy, emphasizing its quasi-improvisatory animated nature with tambourine, side drum, bells and all.

Fig. 179

Folk music

The folk-music revival which had its origins in nineteenth-century nationalism reached one of its most influential phases during the first half of this century. It was feared that the rapid spread of the Industrial Revolution, which filled urban centres with uprooted country people, would bury indigenous musical traditions that were fundamentally agricultural in origin. This is one of the reasons why folk-music collecting and the science of ethnology and, more particularly, ethno-musicology evolved with increasing urgency during the nineteenth century and well into the first quarter of the twentieth. One could say that the folk-music revival came in the nick of time.

Folk music is based on the orally transmitted tradition, some-times over centuries, of country people and as such reflects the very essence of human expression within a nation. Folk music is an important part of the heritage of a country as a spontaneous revelation of a nation's past or, as Vaughan Williams said when defining folksong, 'an individual flowering on a common stem'.

One of the benefits of the folk-music revival was that it served as a means for some composers to create an authentic national musical style. Our interest here, however, focuses on the impact of folk music on modern composers who assimilated it into their complex compositional thinking for its enriching and liberating influence, thus enabling them to express new musical ideas founded on old roots. The term 'liberating influence' should again be seen in the context of the desire of many composers to turn away from the nineteenth-century romantic Austro-German musical hegemony and to find new means of musical expression. For some, folk music played a singular role in achieving these aims. What are the particular characteristics in folk music which fascinated such musicians as Janáček, Stravinsky, Bartók, Kodály, Falla and Vaughan Williams? In short, they may be summarized as follows:

(a) Folksongs are often written in modes (Dorian, Phrygian, Lydian, Mixolydian and so on).
(b) They are also often based on the pentatonic scale (such as C D E G A).
(c) The rhythm is often asymmetric (for example Bulgarian rhythms: 5/8, 7/8).
(d) There is a tendency towards ostinato technique (that is, rhythmic and melodic patterns characterized by trance-inducing repetitions).
(e) The origin of many folksongs collected during the nineteenth and early twentieth centuries goes back to much earlier periods; they represent a continuous link between past and present.

The above contrasts strikingly with the traditional concert repertory, which is tonal, diatonic/chromatic and rhythmically regular, with a preference for symmetry. No wonder that so many modern composers found in folk music invigorating potential for formulating their own styles. The oral transmission of folk melodies has shaped them to a pearl-like perfection. Such melodies are particularly suited to theme and variations or a collection of songs and dances in the form of a suite, which is why composers influenced by folk music so often write variations, suites, fantasies and rhapsodies. These forms suit the somewhat finite and therefore dominating nature of folk music. They allow a composer a certain freedom, and to assemble the folk material in a quasi–improvisatory, rhapsodic manner. Once the easily grasped folk melody is stated and establishes a rapport with the listener, the composer can then set out to unfold its musical potential. The unexpected is founded on the familiar. Examples of this genre are such compositions as Bartók's Dance Suite, George Butterworth's *Shropshire Lad* (rhapsody for orchestra), Delius's *Brigg Fair: An English Rhapsody*,

Fig. 180a ∧ **Fig. 180b** ∨

Holst's *Somerset Rhapsody*, Janáček's Lachian Dances, Kodály's Variations on a Hungarian Folksong ('The Peacock') and Vaughan Williams's three *Norfolk Rhapsodies* and Fantasia on Greensleeves. To illustrate the essence of this style, Fig. 180 gives the complete 'Peacock' tune Kodály used and also the opening nine bars of the eighth variation. Notice that it is a pentatonic tune chiselled by time to ascetic simplicity and has a downward-moving melodic line. Observe the ostinato rhythm and the so-called displaced rhythmic accentuations.

Other popular ways of handling folk themes are to adopt them for solo piano, to set them either individually or as a song cycle with a piano accompaniment and, of course, to arrange them for choral works, including opera. Here are some examples of each:

Piano
Bartók: Hungarian Peasant Songs, Improvisations on Hungarian Peasant Songs
Janáček: National Dances of Moravia

Song setting
Bartók and Kodály: Twenty Hungarian Folksongs
Janáček: A Garland of Moravian Folksongs
Vaughan Williams: Five English Folksongs

Chorus
Bartók: Hungarian folksongs (for mixed choir)
Martinů: *Czech Rhapsody* (cantata)
Stravinsky: Four Russian Peasant Songs (for female voices)

Opera
Janáček: *The Beginning of a Romance*
Kodály: *Háry János, Czinka Panna*

When folk music is absorbed to the extent that it becomes second nature to a composer, it can permeate his or her compositional style with such depth and naturalness that it sounds like the mother tongue. Bartók, Janáček, Stravinsky and Vaughan

Fig. 181

Williams, to mention the most obvious names, have achieved that profound assimilation of folk idioms into their own compositions. Stravinsky's music of the Russian period projects its Russian identity even when actual folk music is not used by him (incidentally, he quotes relatively few folk melodies). Similarly, Bartók's music projects its Hungarian and central European characteristics whether or not he quotes a note from folk sources. The Concerto for Orchestra is a case in point. Composed in 1943 in America, when Bartók was homesick and a dying man, it is a work of synthesis; the Bartókian fusion of the Orient and the West is achieved, but it is Hungarianness which is most evident in the score. He does not rely on quotations of Hungarian folk melodies as his music *is* Hungarian music; it has the authenticity of his mother tongue. The passage in Fig. 181 is taken from the first movement of the Concerto for Orchestra, starting at bar 272. Note the folkish and lyrical simplicity of the melody, the inverted answering phrase at bars 275–7; then the upward-surging melody at bars 278–80 and the falling last three bars, 281–3, which symmetrically end this moving statement. Here Bartók is no longer quoting Hungarian music. It is his music which is Hungarian by virtue of his total absorption of Hungarian and central European folk music.

The influence of popular music

For convenience the term 'popular music' will be applied here to several distinct musical genres, such as waltz, cabaret music, blues, jazz and pop. The merit of this approach is that it enables one to juxtapose so-called serious or concert music – not for qualitative reasons, but for the sake of argument – with the type of music which, though it is now often performed in concert conditions, is by and large characterized by its 'light', diverting quality. Moreover, it gives one a chance to see how far the demarcation lines between these traditionally contrasting groups, light and serious, have been blurred by changing attitudes in evaluating music and, above all, by the influence popular music has exercised on the concert repertory.

In a way music has never lost its ritualistic origin; the divisions which have evolved in music over centuries are largely social superstructures built on a fundamental instinct, that is, man's desire to express his awe, feelings and thoughts in one way or another, be it verbal, visual or acoustic, such as in music. One of the most obvious examples concerning the continuous interchange between secular and sacred, popular and serious music manifests itself in the long history of dance. The suite, for instance, which became one of the most important instrumental forms of the seventeenth and eighteenth centuries, was based on playing a succession of highly stylized old dances, such as the allemande, courante, sarabande and gigue, with other optional dances, such as the bourrée, galliard, gavotte, minuet, passepied, pavan and rigaudon. Many of these popular dances were adopted by the courts and court composers in spite of their more humble origins. A striking example is the sarabande, a dance in slow triple time. It first appeared in the sixteenth century in Spain, where its 'lascivious' nature scandalized such distinguished men as Cervantes and Juan de Mariana. It was eventually banned there by Philip II. In his *Tratato contra los juegos publicos* Juan de Mariana called it 'a dance and song, so lascivious in its words, so ugly in its movements, that it is enough to influence even very honest people'. Yet this is the dance which later inspired Bach in some of his most profound musical statements, not only in his suites and partitas, but also in the final chorus of the *St Matthew Passion*. Bach's use of the sarabande offers us supreme models of musical metamorphosis. Another striking example is the absorption of the Austrian ländler, a peasant dance in slow triple time that was a precursor of the waltz, which eventually superseded it, by many nineteenth-century composers (including Beethoven, Schubert, Chopin, Brahms, Berlioz and Bruckner). Nor was the sarabande the only dance to be banned. The Austrian langaus, in vogue during the late eighteenth century and similar to the ländler or waltz, was forbidden by the Austrian authorities on account of its provocative steps. *Plus ça change, plus c'est la même chose.*

In turning to composers of the late nineteenth century and early part of the twentieth we find that their interest in dance music has an additional dimension when compared with earlier composers. Modern composers used dances, and particularly contemporary dances, because they saw in them a vehicle for rebellion against romanticism. They found delight in deflating the lofty ideas of the romantics, of which Jean Cocteau warned us to be suspicious when he said in his usual witty way, 'Wagner c'est le type de la musique qui s'écoute dans les mains' (Wagner's is the kind of music which one listens to with one's face buried in one's hands) and 'Toute musique à écouter la figure dans les mains est suspecte' (All music which has to be listened to with one's face buried in one's hands is suspect). The vogue for the music of the cabaret, the circus and the café and for jazz and Latin American dances during the period between the 1880s and 1930s was indeed a deliberate move against romanticism, in musical terms an attack on nineteenth-century values, which the avant-garde set out to challenge by mockingly resorting to risqué musical subject-matters. In painting too there was a similar development, and subjects were taken from the ballet, the circus, the café, brothels and prostitutes. In this context the names of Degas, Toulouse-Lautrec, Picasso and Grosz come to mind immediately. This development was associated mainly with Paris. Soon, however, Berlin and Munich joined in the cult of the cabaret, but there it turned markedly political, lampooning the bourgeois in a style which is now largely linked with the collaboration of Brecht and Weill. Popular dance music of all kinds permeates the compositions of this period. For the French, who wanted to stress their own musical identity, this meant a welcome return to their characteristic attitude to music, which emphasizes enlightened *divertissement*.

One of the leading figures in sophisticated entertainment was Satie, himself a cabaret pianist. His strange combination of irony and simplicity, his preoccupation with medieval Christianity and his regular playing in the Chat noir café in Montmartre are all reflected in his compositions. In them one can find a deliberate revival of the church modes; spicy chords based on unresolved sevenths and ninths, as well as the formation of chords on seconds, fourths and fifths; the use of bruitist sonorities (such as gun, whip, typewriter); and his idea of background music, or, as he called it, *musique d'ameublement* (furniture music), which was to exist, like furniture or wallpaper, but should not be listened to in the respectful manner of ordinary concert-goers. As early as 1890 he abandoned bar-lines in his piano composition *Trois gnossiennes*. In these pieces, even more than in the *Trois gymnopédies*, he created quasi-static music, the concept of minimal motion, as if, like a mobile, the music were fixed at a central point. Thus Satie, by tampering with the centuries old notion of progressive motion, the *sine qua non* of Western music, introduced an idea which to this day is practised in the Orient, but had lost its relevance in Western musical thinking as the Gregorian chant lost its dominating role after the Renaissance. Another innovation Satie played with was making duration, instead of pitch, the basis on which music is structured.

His repertory consists largely of piano pieces, among them several dances (such as the three Sarabandes, composed in 1887), many of which have eccentric titles and bizarre commentaries written over the scores: 'like a nightingale with toothache' appears in his composition *Three Dried-up Embryos*; in his *Bureaucratic Sonatina* he states that 'he dreams of promotion'; *Three Pear-shaped Pieces* comprises seven pieces to add to the bewilderment; in *Sports and Diversions* he gives twenty sketches of sporting activities. Together with his few larger-scale works, such as his surrealist ballet *Parade* (subtitled 'Ballet realist' and written in collaboration with Cocteau, Massine, Picasso and Diaghilev's Ballets Russes) and his ascetic rendering of passages from Plato's *Socrates*, his compositions make up an overall picture of a musician of great integrity and far-reaching originality. Fig. 182 is taken from his

Fig. 182

Prélude de la porte héroïque du ciel, in which a gentle modal world is combined with some jazz-like chords (note the absence of bar-lines). In this piece, as in numerous others, the listener is confronted with a strange mixture of nobility and the atmosphere of the café, creating a similar sensation to that of some of Toulouse-Lautrec's paintings or posters. It is worth stressing that this composition was written in 1894, when Brahms was still alive.

Socrate, a symphonic drama for four sopranos and orchestra, consists of three parts, the third of which is devoted to Socrates' death; it was composed in 1919, presumably prompted by the death of Debussy the previous year. Of the two, who influenced the other first is difficult to tell. Although Satie saw in Debussy traces of Wagner-influenced romanticism, one might say that modernism in music came out of their hats. What Debussy thought of Satie's music is perhaps best illustrated by the fact that in 1897 he orchestrated two of the latter's *Gymnopédies*.

The music-hall style had little effect on Debussy's writing, but there are some exceptions, for example the well-known 'Golli-wogg's Cake Walk' from the *Children's Corner* suite for piano. There one finds an uninhibited sound image of the syncopated cakewalk rhythm (see Fig. 183a) and, for good measure, Debussy mockingly introduces Wagner's Tristan motif with almost a giggle and an equally ironic verbal indication, 'avec une grande émotion' (see Fig. 183b). The influence of Debussy and Satie on twentieth-century composers can hardly be overstated and persists to this day.

Fig. 183a ∧　**Fig. 183b** ∨

Satie's impact can be observed not only on Ravel, but also on the members of Les Six, who saw him as the father of many of their own aspirations. Satie wrote the music for the ballet *Relâche: Ballet instantané*, which contains a cinematographic entr'acte; if one looks at the compositions of Auric and his speciality, film music, the influence of Satie's uncomplicated, light, functional writing is detectable. It was almost inevitable that Auric should turn to writing film music, especially for Cocteau's films (*Le Sang d'un poète*, *La Belle et la bête*, *Le Testament d'Orphée* and so on), as he was associated with Les Six. When one considers those compositions of Poulenc that embody the spirit of the café, jazz and the circus, traces of Satie are also evident. This style, which Stuckenschmidt called 'intellectualized variety', can be found in Poulenc's *Rapsodie nègre*, *Cocardes* and the ballet *Les Biches*, in which romantic lyricism is balanced by·his elegant wit and *joie de vivre*. He was a versatile composer and a very fine songwriter, as his settings of the poems of Apollinaire, Cocteau, Éluard, Aragon and Lorca demonstrate.

Milhaud, an immensely prolific member of Les Six, was perhaps the most strongly influenced by Latin American music as well as jazz. This is clear from two of his better-known ballets, *Le Bœuf sur le toit* and *La Création du monde*. The anti-romantic tendency which he fully shared with the group was given expression in such works as his setting of the text of a seed catalogue under the title *Catalogue de fleurs*. The idea of anti-romantic subject-matters in music, which also points back to Satie, gained further expression in Honegger's *Pacific 231* (the name of an American locomotive) and *Rugby*.

It is well known that Debussy did not like to be called an impressionist. Les Six also protested against the label 'modernist', which they judged to be nearly as dangerous as the music of Wagner or the impressionists. But regardless of their protests, their works, carried out with such flair, have characteristics that are irrefutably associated with modern musical developments and irreverent wit. To round off our discussion of Les Six, here is a fragment from the third movement, headed 'Brazileira', of Milhaud's *Scaramouche*, a suite for two pianos. It is a samba in 2/2.

Fig. 184

Stravinsky's dictum that 'rhythm and motion, not the element of feeling, are the foundations of musical art' summarizes the anti-romantic sentiments of the period around the First World War. By giving primary importance to rhythm and motion, he revealed his preoccupation with dance, which is evident in such spectacular works as *Firebird*, *Petrushka* and *The Rite of Spring* (composed between 1909 and 1913). This interest led him to absorb not only ballet, folk dance and dances from the past, but also contemporary dance music and, of course, jazz. Consequently the chamber music style of the jazz band, with its brassy and reedy sounds backed by relentless rhythm (free structure, polyrhythm and syncopation), the interchangeability of major and minor chords, the 'blue' notes and the omission of the string section, added to his (and others') musical development. The jazz craze which finally hit Europe near the end of the First World War found its way into the concert repertory in, as already mentioned, Satie's *Parade* and Milhaud's *Bœuf sur le toit* and *La Création du monde*, and also in Krenek's jazz opera, *Jonny spielt auf*, the first of its kind, Hindemith's *Suite '1922'* for piano and Honegger's Concertino for piano and orchestra. Works that reflect the influence of jazz on Stravinsky are *The Soldier's Tale*, *Rag-time* for eleven instruments, *Piano-rag-music*, Symphonies of Wind Instruments, the *Ebony Concerto* for clarinet and jazz band and the Tango for piano, to mention the most obvious examples. The *Ebony Concerto* was composed as late as 1945, which illustrates the persisting effect jazz had on him. An extract from it is given in Fig. 185.

An interesting cross–Atlantic influence may be traced in the music of Gershwin and Ravel. Popular dances and the songwriting styles of Tin Pan Alley, as well as jazz, were in Gershwin's blood; they represent his musical ancestry. But he also set out to assimilate some aspects of the European concert style. Ravel, on the other hand, was one of the most sophisticated European musical minds of his time and he, like other musicians of the period, playfully absorbed jazz for its exotic, humorous and liberating aspects. In their own ways the two composers succeeded in bridging the gap

B♭ Trumpets

Fig. 185

between light and serious musical styles. Gershwin chose the Liszt-inspired rhapsody and concerto forms, into which he implanted American popular styles – see, for example, his *Rhapsody in Blue*, *An American in Paris*, Piano Concerto in F, Second Rhapsody, 'I got rhythm' Variations and the opera *Porgy and Bess*. Ravel achieved his stylistic fusion in the spirit of French intellectual sophistication which he shared with Debussy, Satie and the leading members of Les Six, though he did not belong to the group. This spirit is evident in his *Boléro*, his Piano Concerto for the left hand, his Piano Concerto in G and the slow movement of his Violin Sonata. In order to give some idea in notational form of what has been argued above, two examples are quoted in Fig. 186, the first from Gershwin's *Rhapsody in Blue* and the second from Ravel's Piano Concerto in G.

Ravel's preoccupation with dance was expressed in what may be his finest orchestral *tour de force*, *La Valse (poème chorégraphique)*, a work in which the waltz, that very epitome of graceful, sensuous, Viennese merry-making, reaches a tragic apotheosis. Ravel started to work on it before the First World War, but completed it

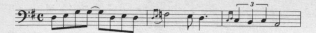

Fig. 186a ∧ **Fig. 186b** ∨

afterwards, in 1920. It could perhaps be seen as a musical reflection of an ending era.

Although the vogue for music halls, nightclubs, jazz and so on settled down after the 1930s, many composers, including ideological ones, carried on turning to popular musical forms for various reasons. Mátyás Seiber, for example, who in his earlier days was one of the first jazz teachers in Europe, was equally at home in light and serious music. His essays in jazz in the late 1920s and early 1930s included two *Jazzolettes* for sextet, and in the late 1950s he collaborated with John Dankworth in a massive piece, *Improvisations*, for jazz band and symphony orchestra.

William Walton brought British modern music in line with Continental developments of the 1920s with his *Façade* (whose well-known theme is quoted in Fig. 187). This 'entertainment' sets a selection of Edith Sitwell's rhythmically recited poems to music played by a small chamber ensemble of six, including percussion.

Fig. 187

The lesser-known Constant Lambert also contributed to this process of modernization. During the 1920s and early 1930s he composed several blues- and jazz-inspired compositions, which are still fun today: *Elegiac Blues*, the Piano Sonata, *The Rio Grande* and the Concerto for piano and wind instruments.

Tippett's interest in jazz, but above all in blues and spirituals, is based not so much on rebellious wit and humour, as is the case with Walton and Lambert, as on the ideological recognition that by using popular idioms he can identify more closely with the suffering of mankind and, in return, the listener can find some immediate foothold, a musical rapport, in what might otherwise be a complex composition. This is made abundantly clear in his adaptation of the Negro spiritual in his secular oratorio *A Child of Our Time*, where he uses it in the manner of a Bach chorale. In his Concerto for double string orchestra blues style is employed most effectively in the second movement (see Fig. 188). Incidentally, it is a work in which Tippett's interest in counterpoint – he himself referred to it as 'a study in polyphony' – Elizabethan music, the concerto grosso style of the baroque era and folk music are convincingly fused. The Third Symphony shows a reliance on 'slow' as well as 'fast' blues. In his third opera, *The Knot Garden*, both jazz and the Negro spiritual gain musico-psychological significance.

Davies, whose parodying enabled him to bring together seemingly incongruous materials (which is, after all, an essential element of parody), succeeded in producing several outrageously witty compositions, among them the *St Thomas Wake: Foxtrot for Orchestra* from the late 1960s. In this immensely amusing piece the original pavan, a popular dance from the sixteenth and seventeenth centuries in duple time (revived by Fauré, Ravel, Vaughan Williams and others), is brought into our century in conjunction with a popular modern dance, the foxtrot. Thus past and present meet in a grotesque *pas de deux*.

In America it was Ives, the pioneering father of modern American music, who liked to mix diverse musical elements in his compositions. These originated from a whole range of sources, such as folk music, hymn-tunes, popular songs and marches, and were fused with the most sophisticated modern compositional

Fig. 188

Fig. 189

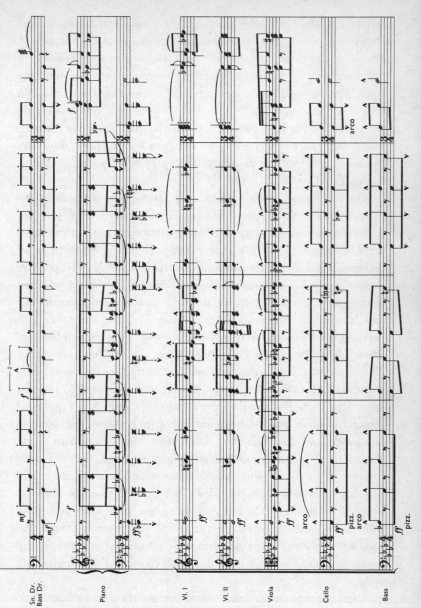

techniques (for example polytonality, atonality, asymmetrical rhythm and collage), virtually paralleling, if not anticipating, European developments. In his music the conservative division of light and serious music is largely blurred by his free-thinking style. The most disparate components are moulded into a sound world very much his own and, moreover, quintessentially American. With him America found its first authentic musical voice. Fig. 189, from Ives's *Three Places in New England*, illustrates the way in which he suddenly utilizes a well-known tune in a sophisticated orchestral score.

Ives was by no means a naïve artist, though he was something of a 'natural' in the sense that his compositional style was not formed out of an ideology. His compatriot Copland, on the other hand, searched for his own language and finally achieved it by incorporating and expressing socio-cultural values in popular music. After his apprenticeship with Nadia Boulanger in Paris during the 1920s he turned his attention to the harmonic, melodic and, above all, rhythmic characteristics of blues and jazz. This meeting with genuine Afro-American music bore fruit in his suite *Music for the Theatre*, the Four Piano Blues and the Piano Concerto. The 1930s was a stern period, best represented by his outstanding Piano Variations. He then started to cultivate a nationalist, popular approach with the clearly stated aim of finding his personal American voice and of bridging the gap between the modern composer and his audience. Copland's encounter with Latin American music, and particularly Mexican music, made a deep impression on his thinking and led him to his first success in this new style, *El salón México*, which is based on popular Mexican tunes (see Fig. 190). The idea of doing the same with American folk tunes soon followed: the titles of the cowboy-song-based ballets *Billy the Kid* (a theme from which is quoted in Fig. 191) and *Rodeo*, and also *Appalachian Spring*, well illustrate this popularizing style.

There are, of course, many more composers who have amalgamated in their concert music popular dance and song styles. This

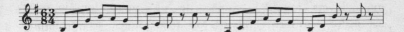

Fig. 190 ∧ **Fig. 191** ∨

is, as they say, an 'ongoing process'. The performances of their music such American minimalist composers (see Chapter Six) as Philip Glass give with their own ensembles are not unlike pop concerts, with regard to both sound and electronic gadgetry.

The aim of this section has been to show the striking influence of popular music of various kinds on the thinking and expression of twentieth-century composers, some of whom are by now regarded as classic.

Non-Western exotic effects

During the nineteenth century nationalist music developed hand in hand with nationalist politics; there was a rapidly growing movement for independence from political oppressors such as the Habsburgs in central Europe. One of the most momentous expressions of nationalist sentiment occurred in the 1848 European revolutions. In terms of music it showed a reaction against the domination of the Austro-German tradition, which, as we have seen, carried on well into the twentieth century. In order to find an independent musical language the nationalist composers turned to the treasure-houses of their national songs and dances, as well as to subject-matters which enabled them to project national characteristics and historic events of importance.

The names of the eminent composers Smetana, Dvořák, Glinka, Borodin, Rimsky-Korsakov and Mussorgsky conjure up in most music lovers' minds a whole series of compositions in which nationalist sentiments relying on folk idioms are prominent. Mussorgsky (a leading member of the so-called Mighty Handful or Russian Five) was perhaps among the most original nationalist composers; his relatively few compositions made a profound impression on both Debussy and Ravel. It should be remembered that in 1889 Rimsky-Korsakov gave a series of concerts in Paris based on the music of the Russian Five and that there was at the same time in France a vogue for all things Russian. Spontaneity and freedom from established formulas, the use of whole-tone (C D E F♯ G♯ A♯ C), pentatonic (C D E G A) and octatonic (C D E♭ F G♭ A♭ A♮ B) scales, recitation influenced by folksong and the Russian Orthodox Church, brilliant orchestral colouring and overall Asiatic *frisson* were some of the striking aspects of Russian music which made Debussy, and others, react with enthusiasm to the Russian Five and, more particularly, to Mussorgsky, of whom he wrote: 'It is like the art of an inquiring savage discovering music step by step through his emotions.' When referring to a 'savage' Debussy could hardly have got nearer to another crucial influence on modern art – what became known as primitivism and eventually evolved into a global interest in non-Western arts and musical styles. The words 'savage', 'primitive' or 'barbaric' should not be interpreted in a derogatory sense. On the contrary, they refer to a freshness and unhindered elemental force with which, it was felt, the West had lost touch. The encounter with the exotic offered a revitalizing cultural blood transfusion to the arts in Europe.

During the twentieth century the West has opened its doors to the rest of the musical world in an unprecedented manner. This interest in Asiatic, African, Middle and Far Eastern, Chinese and Japanese music was substantially helped by rapid developments in communication and travel, especially after the Second World War. But let us go back to the year 1889 when Rimsky-Korsakov was giving concerts in Paris. At the World Fair of that year another momentous musical event took place: an Indonesian group of musicians gave concerts, and for the first time the Western world was able to hear the Javanese and Balinese gamelan (gamelan = orchestra) music. Indonesian music is primarily rhythmic and is played by an ensemble dominated by gongs and tuned metallo-phones. Since that year the sound of metallic and percussive effects has permeated Western music. From Debussy to composers as stylistically diverse as Britten and Boulez, or Bartók and Stock-

Fig. 192

Fig. 193

hausen, all were fascinated and affected by Indonesian music. The influence of the Javanese style may be heard in the second movement of Debussy's String Quartet in G minor, which was completed four years after the World Exhibition; the pizzicato ostinato style is markedly percussive (see Fig. 192). Ten years later, in 1903, Ravel introduced in the second movement of his String Quartet in F Javanese-influenced pizzicato percussive sound effects. Both composers emphasized rhythm in their score markings: Debussy asks for 'Assez vif et bien rythmé' (see Fig. 192) and Ravel for 'Assez vif – Très rythmé' (see Fig. 193). Other pieces by these two composers which show Oriental influence, though not necessarily from Indonesia, are Debussy's 'Fêtes' (*Nocturnes* No. 2) and 'Pagodes' (*Estampes*) and the third movement of Ravel's *Ma mère l'oye* suite, 'Laideronnette, impératrice des pagodes' (see Fig. 194).

Fig. 194

More important than the obvious Oriental pieces, however, are the subtle ways in which elements new to European music have enriched the musical thinking of so many composers with regard to rhythm, melody, harmony and orchestration, as can be observed in the passage from Debussy's *Prélude à l'après-midi d'un faune* in Fig. 195. For reasons of simplicity only the parts of the flute and the harp are given. This illustrates the 'variation in unity' technique of the Javanese orchestra as applied by Debussy. The melodic contour corresponding to the flute is encircled.

Fig. 195

Further fascinating examples may be found in many of Cage's works for prepared piano (for example Sonatas and Interludes). *A Room*, when played on the normal piano, is near in style to that of Bartók, but on the prepared piano it sounds like Balinese music. During the 1930s and 1940s Cage also wrote several compositions for percussive ensembles, such as *Imaginary Landscapes Nos 1–5*, *Double Music* (with Lou Harrison) and *Amores*. These show Oriental preoccupations and influences, which, in his case, embrace more or less the whole of the Orient, that is, Java, Japan, China and India as well as Zen. The above-mentioned Sonatas and Interludes follows the Indian tradition of expressing states of emotion, such as fear or anger, and, as the composer put it, 'their common tendency toward tranquillity'. Cage's relentless philosophizing and radical questioning of music as a means of communica-

tion led him away from the traditionally accepted ways of composing, as we saw in Chapter One when discussing chance music.

A fellow American who in many ways shares Cage's interest in
Oriental music and his experimental outlook is Lou Harrison. In
his music one encounters an eclectic compositional style encompass-
ing the medieval, the serial, chance, fascinating novel sound effects
and Javanese rhythmic ideas all gathered together in order to
project a rather romantic world of sound, as can be heard in his
Piano Concerto. This is a large-scale four-movement concerto
whose second and third movements are influenced by Balinese
gamelan music.

We now turn to two compositions of Stravinsky and Bartók,
who entered Western music with barbaric force. Two examples
are enough to show the elemental rhythmic vitality with which
their music abounds. The first (Fig. 196) is a passage from a piano
piece by Bartók composed in 1911; its telling title is *Allegro barbaro*.
The second illustration (Fig. 197) is from Stravinsky's ballet, a
term not at first seen as appropriate for this ritualistic dance, *The
Rite of Spring* (subtitled *Pictures from Pagan Russia*). It created an
unprecedented scandal at its première in Paris in 1913. The example
is taken from the first part of the work, headed 'The Adoration of
the Earth'. The aural impact of the *Rite* may be equated with the
visual daring of Picasso's *Les Demoiselles d'Avignon* and Matisse's
Danse. With these works a new era of European art was established.
Bartók's interest in Arabic music has already been referred to (see
Chapter One), but there is also evidence that his wide-ranging
studies included Javanese music. The piece quoted in Fig. 198 is
called 'From the Island of Bali' (*Mikrokosmos* Vol. IV No. 109).
The contrasting inner section of this ternary-structured composition evokes with brilliant simplicity the Javanese percussion style.

In the highly complex alchemy of Messiaen's works the exotic
elements derived from Java, India, Greece, birdsongs and mathematical rhythmic calculations are moulded into his personal style
of ecstatically sensuous Catholic mysticism. Traces of the Javanese

Tempo giusto (♩ = 76 - 84)

Fig. 196

Fig. 197

Fig. 198a ∧ **Fig. 198b** ∨

are evident in his scoring for the percussion section, which consists of such instruments as celesta, glockenspiel, vibraphone, gong and percussively applied piano. *Trois petites liturgies de la Présence Divine*, the *Turangalîla-symphonie* and *Couleurs de la cité céleste* are three outstanding examples.

Perhaps even more importantly, Messiaen was influenced by the rhythmic patterns, called 'talas', of India, on which he based his own theory of rhythm. The reader is advised to listen to his piano composition *Quatre études de rythme* and to read his book *Technique of My Musical Language*. In this erudite work he explains his harmonic thinking, which is founded on atonal modes (or scales) within an octave. The modes are arrived at by arranging a series of six to ten pitches. To give two examples, mode 1 is C D E F♯ G♯ A♯ (C), a whole-tone scale. Mode 2, C C♯ D♯ E F♯ G A A♯, is an octatonic scale, which is so characteristic of Messiaen that students wishing to imitate him only have to play around with it to achieve a relatively passable semblance of his music.

By and large modern British composers have been much less affected by Oriental music than their European and American counterparts. Nevertheless, for a few it was inspirational. Holst was interested in Arabic (see, for example, his *Beni Mora*) and Indian music (see *Sāvitri*) and he even learned Sanskrit. Britten's encounter with Javanese music found expression in his ballet *The Prince of the Pagodas*, directly inspired by a visit to the Far East, and in his opera *Death in Venice*. In both cases the choice of tuned percussion ensembles points to the Javanese gamelan.

Equally successful was Britten's involvement with Japanese culture, above all classical Japanese Noh theatre. Its origin goes back to the fourteenth century and is largely associated with a famous Japanese actor and dramatist of that time, Zeami Moto-kiyo. Influenced by Zen, it opposes rationalism and cultivates spontaneity. It is an aristocratic court art based on highly stylized acting performed in drastically simplified scenery, and makes use of dance, masks, mime and discrete sounds. Actors, chorus and musicians all appear together on the stage in a performance which can last for several hours. Britten was impressed with the Noh play *Sumidagawa*, by a medieval playwright Juno Motomasu, in which a mother who has gone mad is in search of her lost son. He saw in it a similarity with medieval English sacred drama. To quote his own words:

Surely the Medieval Religious Drama in England would have made a comparable setting – an all-male cast of ecclesiastics – a single austere staging in a church – a very limited instrumental accompaniment – a moral story? And so we came from *Sumidagawa* to *Curlew River* and a church in the Fens, but with the same story and similar characters, and whereas in Tokyo the music was the ancient Japanese music jealously preserved by successive generations, here I have started the work with that wonderful plainsong hymn 'Te lucis ante terminum', and from it the whole piece may be said to have grown.

Britten's *Curlew River* is a neo-medieval church parable based on Noh theatre. It is a cross-fertilization of the Japanese and the English past, of the Orient and the West.

Other composers influenced by Japan include Cowell, who wrote two concertos for koto (thirteen-stringed zither), Messiaen, whose *Sept haïkaï* are a modern rendering of Japanese court music, and Stockhausen. He has visited Japan on a number of occasions and his creative reaction to Japanese music is evident in several of his compositions:

gagaku ensemble: *Der Jahreslauf*
Japanese percussion: *Telemusik* (a collage of fragments including Japanese percussion music)
ceremonial music and Noh play: *Mantra*, *Inori* and *Licht* (a cycle of seven operas of Wagnerian proportions, still to be completed)

Apart from Messiaen (and, to cross into another field, the Beatles in their famous album *Sgt Pepper* and such songs as 'Love You Too' and 'Within You Without You'), it is some of the American minimalist composers who have benefited most from their encounter with Indian music.

La Monte Young, one of the early minimalists, was captivated by north Indian classical music and decided to take up its study. He mastered classical Indian music playing so well that he was able to perform it with his master, Pran Nath. In 1971 he was honoured with the appointment of director of the Kirana Center for Indian Classical Music. Influenced by the long drone sounds of Indian music as well as the medieval parallel organum, Young evolved a compositional style which expresses a sense of mystic involvement with eternity. Representative works include *Poem for Chairs, Table, Benches, etc.*, *Pre-tortoise Dream Music*, *The Tortoise, His Dreams and Journeys* and *The Well-tuned Piano*, an ongoing work.

Like Young, Terry Riley was influenced by Indian music, and he too became a pupil of Pran Nath in India in order to study the performance of ragas. When comparing Riley's treatment of Indian music with Young's, it is noticeable that it is less mystic. In a pragmatic way he mixes Western musical instruments with Indian ones to create, with the help of a synthesizer, a multicultural musical synthesis. A striking example is *The Medicine Wheel*, in which one of the most Western of ensembles, the string quartet, is combined with, among other things, the sitar and tabla.

Steve Reich showed an early interest in rhythm. He studied the drum in his teens, and became involved with African and Balinese music, which he found congenial to his primarily percussive, rhythm-oriented approach to composition. He discovered that by applying 'phasing', a technique he pioneered with the use of tape recorders, whereby the same recorded voice is played at fractional and varying intervals in 'canon' with itself, a new and exciting musical texture is created. By using this technique and absorbing the essentials of African music and Javanese gamelan music, he has arrived at a synthesis which is based not on imitation but on transformation. Reich is not spicing Western music with Oriental sonorities: he has gone beyond that. A selection of representative compositions to which the reader is directed are *Come Out*, *Piano Phase*, *Drumming*, Music for Eighteen Musicians, *The Desert Music* and *Six Marimbas*.

Another American minimalist composer, Philip Glass, had the good fortune to meet and work with two outstanding Indian musicians, Ravi Shankar and Allah Rukha. This, as he himself put it, was 'a revelation'. It introduced him to a world of music in which rhythm and time are given an entirely different treatment from that of the Western tradition. Glass summed it up: 'In Western music we divide time – as if you were to take a length of time and slice it the way you slice a loaf of bread. In Indian music (and all the non-Western music with which I'm familiar), you take small units or "beats", and string them together to make up larger time values.' Accordingly, Glass builds on his considerable experience and understanding of the music of many places, among them India, as the quotation illustrates, Africa and central Asia. His complex style also owes much to the liberating influence of Cage, to his long-standing involvement with avant-garde theatre and to pop music, whose amplified instruments he himself uses. Like most of the minimalists, Glass has his own band, whose performances on occasion have succeeded in intoxicating the audience as a pop or rock concert might. It should be said that such rock groups as Talking Heads, Pink Floyd and the Police show not only the influence of African and Indian music, but also an affinity with minimalist techniques in their obstinate (ostinato) repetition of short melodic and rhythmic patterns and in their approach to diatonically and modally based melodic constructions.

Finally, let us consider the fact that whereas the music of Japan, Indonesia, India and South America has exercised a direct influence on contemporary musical developments in the West, neither Africa nor China seems to have done so to a comparable extent. With regard to the former, the likely reason for this is that African musical art has entered Europe largely through the tragedy of the slave trade to America, and it is from there that Afro-American music, in the form of spirituals, gospel, ragtime and jazz, has emerged as a potent musical force. As far as China is concerned, there can be little doubt that its traditionally isolationist attitude and the political and cultural oppression that its people have endured have been contributing factors. A notable exception, however, is Cornelius Cardew, whose change from avant-garde artist to Maoist propagandist during the 1970s, a stance he maintained to his death in 1981, offers a sorry picture of the effect of a totalitarian ideology on a gifted musician. For a while he was something of a British John Cage.

The next chapter is devoted to the discussion of isms and stylistic trends from the late nineteenth century onwards. It is hoped that the reader will have a better foundation for understanding these trends after having absorbed this examination of the diversity of musical influences and sources in this century.

CHAPTER SIX

Isms and Styles: *late romanticism, symbolism, impressionism, art nouveau,* japonisme, *pointillism, verismo, expressionism, tonal, atonal and serial expressionisms, serialism, futurism, bruitism, dadaism, surrealism, furniture music,* Gebrauchsmusik, *neoclassicism, folklorism, social realism, collage, music theatre, minimalism*

Music is now so foolish that I am amazed. Everything that is wrong is permitted. SAMUEL SCHEIDT (1587–1654)

When a work of art appears to be in advance of its period, it is really the period that has lagged behind the work of art. JEAN COCTEAU

This chapter surveys the trends in compositional styles since late romanticism. Most of the terms used in defining a period or style in music (the romantic era, impressionism, futurism and so on) have been borrowed from art and literature, so much so that there are some musicologists who question whether it is correct to apply them to music. They argue that it is better to refer to an age or period by defining it through a dominating creative figure (as in 'the age of Beethoven') or by discussing music within a convenient framework of definite historical milestones (for example 'music since the First World War', 'music since the Second World War'). Others argue in favour of some definite musical terms (such as 'the end of tonal music', 'composers of twelve-note music') in order to avoid the possible danger of oversimplifying the stylistic relationships between other arts and music and, above all, to establish independent codes of stylistic references for music. Yet since music functions not in isolation but in interaction with many other factors, be they historical, political, social or artistic, some hold the view that it is quite legitimate to use terms which can evoke the wide spectrum of artistic developments. As Baudelaire put it, 'the arts tend, if not to complement each other, to lend one another new energies'. It is in this spirit that terms which originated in art forms other than music but have now established themselves in general parlance, such as symbolism, impressionism and expressionism, are discussed here.

It is worth bearing in mind that stylistic periods generally overlap. When romanticism was at its peak, symbolism, impressionism and even anti-romantic tendencies were emerging and existing side by side. To be alive in any particular century does not necessarily mean one is stylistically attuned to it. For instance Rakhmaninov, who died in 1943 in America, had nothing to do with modern music. He was the last of the great nineteenth-century Russian romantics and his work remained stylistically untouched by the major changes which took place during his lifetime. Chabrier, however, who died in 1894, displays elements in some of his compositions which in concept are strikingly near to the ideas of Les Six. No wonder that Poulenc, who wrote so pertinently about his music, thought highly of him. The reader is referred to Chabrier's orchestral rhapsody *España* and the *Joyeuse marche*, as well as to his daring piano composition *Bourrée fantasque*. His music sounds modern when compared with Rakhmaninov's, yet he did not live long enough to see the end of the nineteenth century.

The most important isms and styles are dealt with as far as is possible in chronological order, and with reference to the preceding five chapters.

Late romanticism

The late romantics are those composers who emerged roughly after Wagner and whose styles, albeit romantic, were progressive. In several books on the music of the late nineteenth and early twentieth centuries their style is referred to by the following interchangeable terms: 'post-romanticism', 'late romanticism', 'progressive romanticism', 'post Wagner and Brahms' and 'transitory period'. Under these headings authors have tried to assemble the names of composers who worked from the years 1890 to 1910 or so, whose roots were linked to the musical tradition of either Wagner or Brahms and who represented in one way or another a transitory link between them and the twentieth century. On occasions this meant lumping together very strange bedfellows: Mahler, Richard Strauss, Reger, Debussy, Ravel, Puccini, Skryabin, Sibelius and Janáček. Neither Debussy nor Ravel can seriously be seen as 'late romantics' or 'transitory' composers, though certain romantic elements are obvious in their work (interest in nature, childhood, a largely programmatic approach to music and so on). Their works are dominated by particularly modernist tendencies: they radically reinterpreted tonality and general harmonic thinking, they established greater formal freedom, they used new orchestral sonorities and exotic influences and deliberately turned away from Austro-German nineteenth-century romanticism. Be that as it may, some composers, such as Mahler and Richard Strauss, may, indeed, be conveniently categorized as progressive late romantics, since their progressiveness is characterized by an adherence to the 'modernism' of Wagner and Liszt as opposed to the alleged 'conservatism' of Brahms.

This dichotomy between Wagner and Brahms was obsessively emphasized by the nineteenth-century Austrian critic and writer Eduard Hanslick, who saw Brahms as the legitimate heir of the great Austro-German musical heritage. But Zemlinsky, Reger and the young Schoenberg, among others, thought that a fruitful compromise could be made by a creative fusion of the two camps. This younger generation took on board Wagner's chromaticism and weakened tonality and his idea of motivic thinking, or leitmotif technique, as well as a programmatic approach to music and a tendency towards the monumental. From Brahms, on the other hand, they gained a renewed interest in non-programmatic instrumental music, especially chamber music, such as the string quartet. Schoenberg, in an essay written as late as 1947 on 'Brahms the progressive', demonstrated his lasting esteem for Brahms, in whose work he saw evidence of harmonic and rhythmic ingenuity.

Some of the late romantics showed a particularly strong predilection for the music of a number of earlier composers, for instance Mahler for Beethoven, Strauss for Mozart and Reger for Bach. Strauss and Reger were beginning to anticipate developments which, during the 1920s, became known as neoclassicism, and it is easy to overlook the fact that Strauss's opera *Der Rosenkavalier*, modelled on Mozart's operatic style, was completed in 1910. The terms 'late romanticism', though more circumscribed, and 'romanticism' are rather vague, as the romantic is an integral element of music of any period. Moreover, while in literature romanticism was confined mainly to the first half of the nineteenth century, in music it covers roughly the whole century and, with the late romantics, runs well into the twentieth. One might see Mahler's death in 1911 and the works of his last years – *Das Lied von der Erde*, the Ninth and Tenth Symphonies – as good pointers indicating the end of romanticism, though the romantic swansongs of Strauss, the *Vier letzte Lieder*, were completed as late as 1948, a year before his death. The rich musical heritage of the nineteenth century, like its other art forms and political theories, overflowed into our century and, to a certain extent, continues to affect us to this day.

Symbolism

Symbolism was primarily a literary movement which originated in France around 1880. To start with it was mainly cultivated by poets, among them Baudelaire, Mallarmé, Verlaine and Rimbaud; it spread abroad, and may be seen in the works of Edgar Allan Poe, Oscar Wilde and Maeterlinck. By the last decade of the nineteenth century its impact had touched most of the arts and many distinguished figures came under its spell: the painters Munch, Gustave Moreau, Odilon Redon, Gauguin and the Pre-Raphaelites, the sculptor Rodin, the writer Ibsen and the composers Richard Strauss and Bartók. The symbolists saw in Wagner something of a patron saint of their movement, for he represented a myth-maker who fused the totality of all the arts. The results of this process were ceremoniously performed in Bayreuth, a temple of artistic worship, and annually attracted pilgrims from all over Europe and beyond. Poetry and music, but specifically the musicality of poetry, were what occupied the imagination of the symbolists. They could have chosen for their motto the famous statement the essayist Walter Pater made in 1873: 'all art aspires towards the condition of music'. A year later Verlaine, in his *Art poétique*, called for 'De la musique avant toute chose' and dismissed as mere 'literature' everything which did not possess the power of the non-verbal poetry of music. Musicality dominated the practitioners of the symbolist style, a style that encouraged the skill of the suggestive, of reference, obscure symbols, myths and magic. It cultivated a refined sensuality and dream-like disposition; vulnerable states of mind were poetically revealed in unexplained symbols which the reader was left to decipher.

In music the symbolist style is above all evident in Debussy's two compositions *Prélude à l'après-midi d'un faune* and *Pelléas et Mélisande*. It was the extra-musical ideas in a poem by Mallarmé and a play by Maeterlinck which inspired the composer to 'realize' the poetically musical symbolisms of these literary works. In Mallarmé's poem 'Après-midi d'un faune' the faun, awakened from an erotic dream, asks 'Did I love a dream?' He vacillates between dream and reality, returning to the other 'reality' of his dreams at the end of the poem. Debussy's music enhances our ability to decipher the symbolism of the poem by purely musical means. He manages to hint at eroticism, expressed by chromatic and languishing motifs, by using subdued, muted instruments; his style is suggestive rather than explicit. Debussy was arguably as much influenced by the symbolists as by the impressionists.

Bartók's opera *Bluebeard's Castle*, though cross-fertilized by expressionism and folk elements, is a work in which musical symbolism gains dramatic expression. In the castle at the third door leading to Bluebeard's wealth his fourth wife, Judith, cries out, 'Fabulous wealth, infinite wealth!' and the magical orchestral oscillation representing jewellery is overshadowed by a chromatic motif of blood. When the sixth door is opened and Judith is confronted by a lake filled with 'tears and weeping', Bartók introduces a shiver-inducing series of arpeggios and the blood motif of a semitone (in this case G–G♯) ominously reappears.

Impressionism

The term 'impressionist' was established after an exhibition in Paris in 1874, where Monet's painting *Impression: soleil levant* was first shown. The critic Louis Leroy, who did not like the work and was unsympathetic to the exhibition as a whole, derisively referred to it as 'impressionist'. The word stuck, and became the label of one of the most important modern movements in art. The style is characterized by the avoidance of sharp contours and the use of dabs of colour without much preparatory drawing to convey an impression of the interplay of lights and colours. The results were very different from the photograph-like pictures of the 'romantic realists' so venerated by most people of the time.

There were eight impressionist exhibitions between 1874 and 1886, at which the bulk of the works of Monet, Renoir, Sisley, Pissarro, Cézanne, Degas and Morisot were presented. The dates are significant as they correspond to the formative years of Debussy, who was to write a series of compositions showing the influence of impressionism. Extra-musical subject-matters (painterly and poetic ideas expressed by musical means), subdued orchestration (soft dynamics, frequent use of mutes and so on) and blurring are evident, as are a predilection for nuance and evocation, for drifting harmonies rather than dialectic progressions. His work

also featured florid, arabesque-like melodic and rhythmic utterances, and the projection of refined sensuousness. These qualities
can be found in *Printemps* (1887), *Petite suite* (1886–9), *Prélude à
l'après-midi d'un faune* (1892–4), *Nocturnes*: 'Nuages', 'Fêtes', 'Sirènes' (1897–9), *La Mer* (1903–5), *Images: Gigues, Ibéria, Rondes de
printemps* (1905–12) and several of his piano compositions, such as
'Des pas sur la neige', *Préludes* Bk 1 (1909–10).

Art nouveau

During the 1890s a new movement, art nouveau, made itself felt
in both Europe and America. Its roots lay in symbolism and to a
certain extent in decorative aspects of impressionism, as well as in
renewed interest in the Gothic (see, for example, the work of
William Morris). It was particularly successful in the realm of
architecture, interior decoration and book illustration, the best-
known practitioner of which was Beardsley, who represents the
style *par excellence*. How far this ornamental style was transferred
to music is open to debate. Nevertheless, Debussy's *Deux arabesques*
for piano and his setting of three prose poems by Pierre Louÿs,
Chansons de Bilitis, and Richard Strauss's opera *Salome*, based on
the text of Oscar Wilde (which, incidentally, was superbly illustrated by Beardsley in 1894), are works which show at least some
leaning towards art nouveau.

Japonisme

The impressionists also contributed substantially to the popularization of Japanese art and to the development of a virtual craze for
anything from Japan. In France this became known as *japonisme*.
We know that in 1886 a French periodical, the *Paris illustré*,
dedicated an entire edition to Japan. Europe discovered the works
of Hokusai and Utamaro. *Japonisme* made a deep impression on

several artists of the time, namely Manet, Monet, Van Gogh and Gauguin. Debussy, an ardent collector of Japanese prints, used a picture of waves from a Hokusai print for the cover of the score of his orchestral poem *La Mer*. This work is in three movements, each with a picturesque title: 'De l'aube à midi sur la mer', 'Jeux de vagues' and 'Dialogue du vent et de la mer'. There can be little doubt that 'Poissons d'or', from the second set of *Images*, is a musical response to the French *japonisme* of the time.

These digressions into art nouveau and *japonisme* are intended to illustrate the complexity of stylistic influences, together with their overlapping nature, and to give some idea of the cumulative way in which new schools of thought mushroomed during the last decades of the nineteenth century and in the early twentieth. Paris was the centre of the intellectual ferment of this period, in which exotic influences from Russia, Japan and Indonesia met the avant-garde of Western culture to such powerful effect.

Pointillism

The term 'pointillism' was again adopted from fine art. By the 1890s some painters felt dissatisfied with the informality of impressionism and reacted against an art style which, in their eyes, was slowly leading to a dead end. This led Seurat and Signac to develop a scientifically based style, pointillism, which consists of painting with thousands of dots of pure, unmixed colour. These dots are automatically merged by our eyes, enabling us to see colours and forms known as optical mixtures. Although this shimmering technique was not unfamiliar to earlier artists, it was these 'pointillists', also called 'neo-impressionists' or 'divisionists' (they themselves preferred the latter term), who exploited it to the full. Perhaps the best-known examples are *Sunday Afternoon on the Island of La Grande Jatte* by Seurat and *Île de la Cité* by Signac. In his book *From Eugène Delacroix to Neo-Impressionism* (1899) Signac wrote:

One can say that, generally speaking, a Neo-Impressionist work is more harmonious than an Impressionist one, one of the reasons being that because of the way contrasts are always observed, there is more harmony in the details. There is also greater harmony in general effect, and a kind of 'moral harmony' too because the composition is based on aesthetic principles and the language of colours. Impressionism has none of this ... It is not a question of talent but of technique, and no lack of respect is implied when we say that Neo-Impressionist technique assures integrity of colour, luminosity and harmony better than the Impressionist does.

Whatever we may think of 'moral harmony', Signac's statement makes it clear that the neo-impressionists felt that in their works they had gone beyond the impressionists and that their technique was more rationally based.

The term 'pointillism' was borrowed by many writers on music to describe this dotted technique when applied to sound. It is achieved by writing passages of detached notes rather than a flowing melody. The composer who immediately comes to mind in this context is Webern. Even in the theme of his 'late-romantic' work the Passacaglia in D minor Op. 1 a pointillist texture is apparent. In both his atonal and his serial compositions (for example the Six Bagatelles Op. 9 and the Symphony Op. 21) this fragmented instrumental style, combined with concentrated brevity, became something of a personal insignia. After the Second World War composers went further with pointillism, recognizing in Webern's mosaic-like texture new ways in which traditional musical thinking could be challenged. Stockhausen's *Kreuzspiel*, Boulez's *Marteau sans maître* and Ligeti's *Nouvelles aventures* are good starting points for the reader who is unfamiliar with this technique.

Verismo

This term is used in connection with Italian opera of the late nineteenth century. It defines an operatic style in vogue at the time when 'realistic', or 'truthful', and often violent subject-matters were chosen from everyday life, corresponding to the literary realism of the period (see, for example, the novels of Émile Zola). The trouble with the labels 'verismo', 'realism' and 'naturalism' is that art is by its very nature artificial, and realism can exist only in a stylized manner on the stage; that artistic realism is a projected semblance of the real. But regardless of this ambiguity, some works can be seen as representative of the verismo style, especially Mascagni's *Cavalleria rusticana*, Leoncavallo's *I pagliacci* and Puccini's *Tosca*.

Expressionism

Expressionism began in France with Van Gogh and others, and had some affinity with the short-lived fauve movement of Derain, Vlaminck and Rouault. The Germanic and Scandinavian countries, however, found the style particularly congenial to their temperament, and it was in Germany and Norway that the movement flourished in the fine arts, literature and music. The fauvist *Salon d'automne* exhibition in 1905 was paralleled by the group *Die Brücke* in Dresden, which contained such artists as Ernst Ludwig Kirchner and Erich Heckel. This was followed by the founding of another group, *Der Blaue Reiter*, in Munich in 1911. Members included the eminent modern artists Kandinsky, Macke, Nolde and later Klee. These two groups represented the most important manifestation of modernism in Germany before the First World War, though it was a Norwegian, Munch, who excelled in the expressionist idioms to the point of neurotic frenzy. Characteristic of the style is the use of violent colour, manneristic distortions of lines and an obsessive preoccupation with the extreme emotional states of anxiety, love, hate, jealousy, fear, sex, degradation and violence – in short, a preoccupation with the dark labyrinths of the human psyche as mapped out by Freud and others.

Expressionist literature explored similar themes. The names that come to mind are Strindberg, Trakl, Wedekind, Toller and Kafka.

In the works of these authors a nightmarish vision of the human condition, centring on suffering and victimization, is thrust upon the unsuspecting reader. Musical expressionism is associated largely with Schoenberg and his disciples, above all two of his best-known pupils, Berg and Webern. In music there are three distinctive kinds of expressionism: tonal, atonal and serial.

Tonal expressionism

This term refers to music in which the expressionist ideas as described above are projected through a medium still based on tonality, however chromatic the harmonic and melodic style may be. A most representative example is Schoenberg's monodrama *Erwartung* Op. 17, a work of great intensity. A woman has a rendezvous with her lover in a forest at night. Searching for him, she stumbles over his murdered body. In the final scene she talks to him in ecstasy as if he were still alive. Traditional tonal structure is abandoned, though a fundamental reference to D minor is maintained, even if in a blurred way. The key of D had a special significance for Schoenberg during his first, tonally oriented period: two of his early string quartets were in that key, as was his symphonic poem *Pelleas und Melisande*.

The earlier *Verklärte Nacht* Op. 4, originally written for a string sextet, but arranged in 1917 (and revised in 1943) for a string orchestra, is in D minor and ends in D major. Here too the programmatic nature of the work is striking, inspired as it was by a poem of Richard Dehmel. A woman is wandering with her lover on a moonlit night and tells him that she is pregnant by another man who meant nothing to her. She is tormented by shame and guilt. Her true love tells her that she is forgiven and that because of her he loves the child as if it were his own. Through his love he is morally and emotionally transfigured as they ecstatically kiss each other. In this early work Wagnerian chromaticism and Tristanesque intoxicated spiritualization are clearly detectable, particularly in the closing bars. Far from being derivative, however, it is a truly Schoenbergian late-romantic and tonal-expressionistic composition of great passion and beauty.

Atonal expressionism

The real – one could say 'natural' – language for expressionism in music is atonality, and ultimately serial atonality. Again it was Schoenberg who led the way and who was entirely at home with the aims of the movement; he was quite a capable expressionist painter, as his blue self-portrait illustrates. As far as his music is concerned, he himself referred to his three stylistic periods, which can be dated roughly as follows:

(a) tonal (that is, late romantic and tonal expressionism): up to 1908
(b) atonal (atonal expressionism): 1908–21
(c) serial (serial expressionism): from 1921

When looking at the serial period it must be noted that some of his works, for instance the Piano Concerto, completed in 1942, incorporate the idea of 'romantic serial expressionism'. That Schoenberg's compositions remained steeped in romanticism is not in doubt. The unresolved contradiction of his genius was the fact that behind the revolutionary compositional ideas, such as the 'heretical' abandonment of tonality, which brought about a most profound division in Western music, lurked a man with an incorrigible late-romantic and traditionalist temperament. He suffered a lack of recognition for his romanticism, though at times it seems to be practically bursting out of his atonal and atonal-serialist compositions. He admitted to being 'a conservative who was forced to be a revolutionary'. Occasionally he allowed himself a return to tonality, as in his Variations on a Recitative for organ, which are again in his favoured key of D minor.

But to return to atonal expressionism, one of the most striking examples is Schoenberg's *Pierrot lunaire*, a melodrama for female voice and chamber ensemble comprising piano, flute, piccolo, clarinet, bass clarinet, violin, viola and cello. It is a cycle of twenty-one songs based on the German translation of French poems by Albert Giraud and is performed in the *Sprechgesang* style. Although its first performance took place in 1912, the ghostly voice of the moondrunk Pierrot to this day elicits extreme reactions from some listeners.

A pianist of even modest ability can find pleasure and learn about the expressionist style by playing through some of the easier of his Six Little Pieces Op. 19. These are characteristic pearls of the atonal-expressionist repertory.

Serial expressionism

Serial expressionism refers to the application of the serial technique to expressionist musical statements. It has already been suggested that atonality, as well as serial atonality, and the expressionist style were made for each other, but perhaps therein lies their limitation and vulnerability: even today concert-goers are often alienated by the manneristic world of dissonant expressionist sound effects. With a little effort, however, it is possible not only to come to terms with, but even to like several of the works written in this style. Berg's opera *Lulu*, referred to in Chapter Three, and Webern's often epigrammatic compositions, whether written in atonal or serialized atonal styles, are to be recommended.

Serialism

As serialism has already been discussed in earlier chapters, it is sufficient simply to summarize the most important points here. Serial music is one of the most radical twentieth-century musical developments. Its starting point is atonality, but, unlike atonality, serialism is an organized system. The randomness of extreme chromaticism and atonality was formalized by Schoenberg into a system whereby a series of twelve notes serves as a chromatic melody and harmony for the whole composition. A series thus constructed can be played backwards, in inversion and so on. Schoenberg's Piano Suite Op. 25, for example, is based on the following series or twelve-note row: E♮ F♮ G♮ D♭ G♭ E♭ A♭ D♮ B♮ C♮ A♮ B♭. This system was developed further by introducing the serialization of duration and rhythm, among other things, which is called total serialization; in partial serialism fewer than twelve notes are chosen. One of the best introductions to serialism is Berg's Violin Concerto. Once that work is absorbed, other compositions, however complex, will seem easier to appreciate.

Futurism

The term 'futurism' first appeared in an article written by the Italian Marinetti, 'The Founding and Manifesto of Futurism', which was published in *Le Figaro* in Paris in 1909. It was neither a French nor a German modernist movement, but a vigorously Italian one. It flourished for about ten years in all, from Marinetti's first manifesto in 1909 until 1919. During this time the members of the movement published several manifestos, whose tone is one of aggressive optimism: they display a fanatical enthusiasm for the speed and power of the modern scientific age, as symbolized by the car and the aeroplane, a glorification of war for its purging power and an insistence on the abolition of the past for the sake of the new. We have already seen in Chapter Four that the futurists' reaction to music was in favour of everything that was modern. As Marinetti put it, 'We will destroy the museums, libraries, academies of every kind, will fight moralism, feminism, every opportunistic or utilitarian cowardice ... Art, in fact, can be nothing but violence, cruelty, and injustice.' A year later, in the manifesto *Futurist Painting: Technical Manifesto 1910*, signed by five futurists (Boccioni, Carra, Russolo, Balla and Severini), the following statement was made: 'All is conventional in art. Nothing is absolute in painting. What was truth for the painters of yesterday is but a falsehood today. We declare, for instance, that a portrait must not be like the sitter, and that the painter carries in himself the landscape which he would fix upon his canvas.' This was obviously a movement of the now, the revolutionary young, as Marinetti suggested: 'The oldest of us is thirty: so we have at least a decade for finishing our work. When we are forty, other younger and stronger men will probably throw us in the wastebasket like useless manuscripts – we want it to happen!'

The futurists' interest touched upon every aspect of the arts, including, of course, music. The Italian composer who joined the movement was Pratella. His *Manifesto of Futurist Musicians* appeared in 1910, and it too addressed itself to the young:

I appeal to the young. Only they should listen, and only they can understand what I have to say. Some people are born old, slobbering spectus of the past, cryptograms swollen with poison. To them no words or ideas, but a single injunction: the end.

I appeal to the young, to those who are thirsty for the new, the actual, the lively.

Among those composers who, for various reasons, gained Pratella's esteem are Wagner, Strauss, Debussy, Mussorgsky and Sibelius. He also includes Glazunov and Elgar, of whom he wrote:

In England, Edward Elgar is cooperating with our effort to destroy the past by pitting his will to amplify classical symphonic forms, seeking richer ways of thematic development and multiform variations on a single theme. Moreover, he directs his energy not merely to the exuberant variety of the instruments, but to the variety of their combination of effects, which is in keeping with our complex sensibility.

No doubt this would have surprised Elgar. Pratella ends his manifesto with eleven conclusions, the first of which states the desire to 'convince young composers to desert schools, conservatories and musical academies, and to consider free study as the only means of regeneration'.

Those wishing to read these manifestos in full are referred to the splendid Thames and Hudson publication *Futurist Manifestos*, edited by Umbro Apollonio. But our main concern here is the futurists' contribution to music. Pratella supported the ideas of atonality, the use of quarter tones, irregular rhythmic structures and the like. The distinguishing feature of the futurists is their preoccupation with noise, with the concept that in a modern age, characterized by advanced technology, noise is a legitimate way of expressing contemporary ideas in sound. While Schoenberg talked of the 'emancipation of dissonance', the futurists went further, fostering the emancipation of noise. Luigi Russolo, a painter and prominent member of the futurists who was equally involved with music, believed that all kinds of sound sources were acceptable material for a composition. Thus the futurists were propagating and practising certain developments in modern music which came to fruition only many decades later in the form of *musique concrète* and, ultimately, electronic music. Russolo, in his manifesto of 1913, *The Art of Noises*, stated: 'Today music, as it becomes continually more complicated, strives to amalgamate the most dissonant, strange and harsh sounds. In this way we come even closer to noise-sound.' In the same manifesto he gave a list of the six

families of noises of the Futurist orchestra which we will soon set in motion mechanically:

1	2	3	4	5	6
Rumbles	Whistles	Whispers	Screeches	Noises	Voices of
Roars	Hisses	Murmurs	Creaks	obtained	animals
Explosions	Snores	Mumbles	Rustles	by	and men:
Crashes		Grumbles	Buzzes	percussion	Shouts
Splashes		Gurgles	Crackles	on metal,	Groans
Booms			Scrapes	wood,	Shrieks
			Skin	Howls	
			Stone	Laughs	
			Terracotta	Wheezes	
			etc.	Sobs	

We know that Debussy was fascinated with the aims of this movement, as were Honegger, Alexandr Mosolov, Prokofiev, Varèse and Schaeffer. The futurists did indeed live up to their name.

Bruitism

It became popular to refer to the use of noise in art music as bruitism (from the French *bruit* = noise) and it is therefore a legitimate word to employ in the context of the futurists and their subsequent followers. The following compositions serve as an introduction to the futurist and bruitist approach: Satie's *Parade*, Antheil's *Ballet mécanique* and Varèse's *Ionisation*, *Intégrales* and *Poème électronique*.

Dadaism

By randomly inserting a pen-knife into a dictionary a group of like-minded anarchist artists came across the word 'dada', which in French means 'hobby-horse'. This then became the name of a movement which paralleled the futurists – with whom the artists had a strong affinity – and paved the way to another important development, surrealism. Dada was launched in Zurich during the First World War, and flourished from 1915 to 1922. It adopted a deliberately provocative stance, characterized by shock tactics and buffoonery, intended to shake the general public from its philistine complacency.

Marcel Duchamp, a leading figure in the movement, said: 'Dada is the non-conformist spirit which has existed in every century, every period since man is man.' The dadaist style is superbly represented in Duchamp's works, notably the provocative urinal called *La Fontaine*, but none encapsulates the style to greater effect than the notorious *Mona Lisa*, to whose enigmatic smiling face he added a beard and moustache, as well as the obscene title LHOOQ, which reads 'Elle a chaud au cul'. In confronting us with a naughty schoolboy's graffiti Duchamp's aim was to de-mythologize the original, and also to undermine centuries of tra-ditional values.

In literature the dadaists experimented with nonsense, emphasiz-ing the aural and rhythmic elements of a poem, for example, at the cost of meaning. They also experimented with chance and collage by taking words found at random and sticking them together without any logical coherence. Like the futurists, the dadaists were interested in the concept of 'simultaneity' (that is, the presentation of more than one event at the same time, which is achieved by reciting independent texts simultaneously). This suited the dadaists particularly well as they saw life as illogical and chaotic.

As far as music is concerned, the dadaists largely followed the futurists. They were ideologically suspicious of harmony, and so supported the idea of 'noise-music' and cacophony. Dada had much less impact on music than on the arts and literature. Neverthe-less, in the verbal as well as musical tomfoolery of Satie and Cage, dadaist influences, or at least affinities, are quite evident. As Tristan Tzara, one of the movement's founders, put it, 'Dada is a state of mind.'

Surrealism

It was Apollinaire who, as early as 1917, first used the term 'surrealist', but it was another French poet, André Breton, who conceptualized and sharpened it into a new and significant move-ment between the two world wars. Initially it largely comprised former members of the defunct dadaist movement, which ceased in 1922. The basic tenet of surrealism, as expressed in Breton's manifesto in 1924, is an entirely revised interpretation of reality which gives free rein to the subconscious. The direct influence of

Freud, whose analytical theories Breton was familiar with, is of paramount importance to surrealist thinking, as can be seen from the following statement by Breton:

. . . purely psychic automatism through which we undertake to express, in words, writing, or any other activity, the actual functioning of thought, thoughts dictated apart from any control by reason and any aesthetic or moral consideration. Surrealism rests upon belief in the higher reality of specific forms of associations, previously neglected, in the omnipotence of dreams, and in the disinterested play of thinking.

Surrealism is the art of the dream, but also of the nightmare, and as such it is related to expressionism. Irrational images are obtained from the patient's or the artist's unhindered recollection of a dreamed or hallucinated experience, the rendering of which needs to be based on free-flowing accounts. These accounts are generally written down (when they are known as automatic texts), but any other way of expressing or projecting a dream world (such as painting) is equally legitimate. For this reason Breton stressed that 'automatism, inherited from the mediums, remains one of the two major trends of surrealism'.

To start with it was in poetry that surrealism came to the fore, in the works of Breton, Éluard, Aragon and Artaud. But the visual arts soon followed with such notorious characters as Chirico, Dali, Ernst and Magritte, to mention only a few of the most outstanding practitioners of this style. In the world of film, Buñuel's *Un chien andalou* established itself as a remarkable example of how this relatively new art form could be explored in surrealist terms.

Surrealism did not have the same impact on music as impressionism and expressionism, though composers have set surrealist poems to music with most fruitful results. Poulenc, for instance, had a lifelong admiration for some of the surrealist poets, above all Éluard, whose nine poems entitled *Tel jour, telle nuit* he set to music to great effect. Equally successful is his setting of Éluard's brilliant evocation of seven painters, *Le Travail du peintre*: Picasso,

Chagall, Braque, Gris, Klee, Miró and Villon. To pick one example, Poulenc's witty piano accompaniment, together with the playful melody, superbly complements Éluard's poem on Marc Chagall, of which the first stanza is:

> Ass or cow cock or horse
> even the skin of a violin
> a singing man or a single bird
> agile dancer with his wife.

One of the most striking surrealist collaborations between poet and composer came about well after the Second World War in 1954, when Boulez set to music three of René Char's expressionist–surrealist poems *Le Marteau sans maître*. The nine movements are based on a twelve-note set (E♭ F♮ D♮ C♯ B♭ B♮ A♮ C♮ G♯ E♮ G♮ F♯), which is used without adhering to the serial technique in its orthodox form. Another fascinating aspect of this composition is the way in which Boulez separates, blends and finally engulfs the vocal line with the orchestra by 'reducing' the singers to a textless vocalization. It is not far-fetched to suggest that what *Pierrot lunaire* is to expressionism and atonality, *Le Marteau sans maître* is to surrealism and free serialism; both are milestones in which poetry and music jointly project images in manifestly twentieth-century styles.

Neither Poulenc nor Boulez, however, is a surrealist composer, though they were affected by its poetry. The Argentine Mauricio Kagel, on the other hand, composes in a consistently surrealist manner. Kagel resents being labelled, yet his art inescapably reminds us of aspects of expressionism, dadaism and, most of all, surrealism, the style which comes the nearest to his temperament. He belongs belatedly to the surrealist fraternity of Breton, Dali and Buñuel. It is not by chance that in 1982 he came to write music for a reissue of a surrealist silent film of 1928, *Un chien andalou* by Buñuel and Dali. His wide-ranging interests include literature, theatre, film and music, and the ways in which these art forms interact. For him music is only a part of the totality of available forms of expression, but it holds a key position in his scheme. Consequently Kagel's approach to theatre or film is musical, while his approach to music may be, when he wishes, theatrical and visual. His compositions, whether written for purely instrumental music, music theatre or film, are characterized by originality of imagination, wit and a twisted sense of ironic humour. In his works everything can contribute to music-making, from sighing, as in *Siegfried/P*, to the tapping of walking-sticks, as in *Pas de cinq*, and the rhythmically banged chair in *Dressur*.

His interest in silent and surrealist films in general, but in particular those made by Buñuel, and his ideas about the inter-relationship of the arts made him turn to film-making. In Kagel's films music plays such an important role that they could just as well be regarded as musical compositions. Since both forms rely heavily on time sequence – one, being visually perceived, has the advantage of being able to deal with concrete ideas while the other, being abstract, communicates more directly with feelings – Kagel offers a synthesis of music and film. *Antithèse* (1965) was the first of a series of now nearly twenty films that realize this synthetic approach. The music is based on electronic sound effects which blend in with the manic behaviour of a technician, who, on entering a studio packed with abandoned machines of all kinds (record players, radios, tape recorders and so on), goes berserk. *Match* is surrealist chamber-cum-film music in which two cellists are pitted against each other in front of an umpire who is playing percussion instruments and adjudicates in this bizarre musical contest.

Hallelujah is perhaps one of his densest compositions and the most indebted to Buñuel's *Un chien andalou* in terms of surrealist technique and imagery. It has several layers, combining the humor-ous with the near nightmarish. A particularly clever idea is his adoption of a style reminiscent of an anatomy lesson: medical statements concerning the function of the larynx modulate into singing practice which makes use of the word 'Hallelujah'. It is real surrealist fantasy. Kagel's facility for elegant mockery was bound to find a musical outlet. The victim was Beethoven in *Ludwig van*, a surrealist romp with the music of Beethoven in which Kagel shows the distortion brought about by time between Beethoven's period and ours. It is humour – an aspect of surrealism much less commented upon than it deserves – that makes Kagel's work highly entertaining.

Furniture music

As the concept of *musique d'ameublement* (furniture music) has already been discussed, it is sufficient here to remind the reader that the term, originating from Satie, described music written to be played in the background. This stood in contrast to the nineteenth-century tradition of music composed for attentive concert audiences and was a deliberate attempt to deromanticize music. In 1920 Satie and Milhaud jointly composed *Musique d'ameublement* for a small ensemble.

Gebrauchsmusik

Whereas furniture music is intended to be utilitarian in the sense that it blends in with other activities, *Gebrauchsmusik* (utility music) is meant to be earnestly practical: it is written with some useful purpose in mind, be it didactic, political or whatever. It became popular, especially in Germany, during the 1920s and 1930s and adopted an anti-romantic attitude: while the romantics waited for inspiration in order to express their individualism, the composers of *Gebrauchsmusik* set about writing in a craftsman-like, practical, no nonsense, 'let's deliver the goods in time' manner, working as would a tailor or a carpenter. Their example was Bach, who every week served his congregation with a cantata. They were suspicious of the romantic notion of genius, and preferred to project an image of daily work in the service of the community. Although at the time several composers were involved, including Weill, Krenek and Eisler, the term is now usually applied only to Hindemith (though he disowned it), as it was he who systematically composed works of graded difficulty and of diverse instrumental combinations for both amateur and professional players.

Neoclassicism

To some artists, the First World War brought a certain sobriety. One of the most noticeable changes can be observed in Busoni, once the avant-garde wizard, who in his revolutionary essay *Sketch for a New Aesthetic of Music*, published in 1907, advocated total freedom for the composer. After the war, however, he calmed down and called for the 'reconquest of serenity'. He started to propagate the idea of 'young classicism'. Neoclassicism was already in the air, both in theory and in practice, before the war and became increasingly evident after it. Indeed, between the two world wars neoclassicism evolved into one of the most influential movements of our century.

In contrast to most of the stylistic developments discussed so far, neoclassicism was not derived from other art forms. As we saw in Chapters Three and Five, it was primarily a musical movement in which several composers set out to revive the musical forms and textures of the pre-romantic era. They hoped to regain the clarity and objectivity which they felt had been lost during the nineteenth-century romantic period. The term 'neoclassicism' has been used by both composers and musicologists in a rather flexible manner, denoting not only a return to Haydn and Mozart, but also a movement back to Bach and before him, as well as 'clarté latine' when applied by the French or Italians. By returning to the compositional procedures of the seventeenth and eighteenth centuries, composers aimed to absorb classical ideas within a new modern context rather than to copy, write pastiche or parody. It is for this reason that such works as Prokofiev's Classical Symphony and Stravinsky's *Pulcinella* are now justifiably seen as noteworthy, playful stylistic experiments. Delightful as they are, they are nevertheless inspired pastiches, pointing to a new direction. As Stravinsky explained much later in his conversations with Robert Craft (*Expositions and Developments*), 'Pulcinella was my discovery of the past, the epiphany through which the whole of my late work became possible. It was a backward look, of course – the first of my love affairs in that direction – but it was a look in the mirror too.' For Stravinsky the change from his Russian period (*c.* 1909–20) to neoclassicism (*c.* 1920–55) coincided with his 'loss of Russia and its language of words as well as of music'. There can be little doubt that his search for a new style in the firm foundation of a classical past was the search of an uprooted man for new roots. In his and other composers' hands, neoclassicism – that is, the revival of classical formal principles without the tonal implications on which they were based – became an extremely forceful movement. It is in the light of the above definition that even such composers as Schoenberg, whose atonal and serial harmonic thinking differs so drastically from that of the classical diatonic tonal world, may be seen as composing neoclassical works, among them the Piano Suite, Third String Quartet, Cello Concerto and String Quartet Concerto, which took Handel for a model.

To return to Stravinsky, his neoclassical period brought to fruition several masterpieces. In these his tonally based contrapuntal and instrumental mastery and his genius for rhythmic inventiveness, which was largely founded on Russian folk music, gained full expression. In the field of rhythm a remarkable amalgamation of the baroque style and his own Russian and modern background was achieved. He himself stated in *Conversations* (by Stravinsky and Craft): 'Dotted rhythms are characteristic eighteenth-century rhythms: my use of them in works of that period, such as the introduction to my Piano Concerto, are conscious stylistic references. I attempted to build a new music on eighteenth-century classicism, using the constrictive principles of that classicism and even evoking it stylistically by such means as dotted rhythms.' Accordingly, some of Stravinsky's scores from his neoclassical period even look like baroque scores, but, of course, they sound like Stravinsky. A most memorable example illustrating this point is the second movement of his Symphony of Psalms; but other pieces in which baroque or classical musical procedures and patterns were employed are plentiful, notably his Concerto for piano and wind instruments, for which several of Bach's works, for instance the Brandenburg Concertos and the Italian Concerto for solo keyboard, served as models. His Octet for Wind Instruments is related to the baroque overture (sinfonia) as well as Bach's Two-part Inventions. (It was this baroque style which, incidentally, inspired Bartók so movingly in the second movement of his Third Piano Concerto.) In the Sonata for piano Stravinsky blended Bach's polyphony with Beethoven's piano sonata style. It should be noted that in Stravinsky's hands neoclassicism could even embrace a homage to Tchaikovsky, as in his ballet *The Fairy's Kiss*.

In *Oedipus rex*, an opera–oratorio, Stravinsky turned to the classical drama of Sophocles, where he found mythological significance and, in Oedipus' character, tragic grandeur. Instead of the original Greek text, however, Stravinsky chose the Latin because of its long-standing ritualistic connotations: 'What a joy it is to compose music to a language of convention, almost ritual, the very nature of which imposes a lofty dignity!' As always with Stravinsky, rhythm is one of the most fundamental forces in this dark tragedy; the action on the stage is strikingly restricted, almost static, creating an inner tension that the rhythm accentuates. It is worth pointing out that the expression of ritual in musical terms with diverse manifestations (from *The Rite of Spring*, *The Wedding*, *Oedipus rex* and the Symphony of Psalms to the sacred works of his serial period, such as *Canticum sacrum*, *Threni* and *Requiem Canticles*) was one of Stravinsky's major preoccupations. Although several composers besides Stravinsky have adopted the neoclassical style, including Honegger, Milhaud and Hindemith, it is the music of his second period which exemplifies the main trend of neoclassicism. This is why particular emphasis has been given to some of his neoclassical compositions. Familiarity with these will enable the reader to understand better other, perhaps less obviously neoclassical works.

Folklorism

This heading refers to those compositions which in one way or another were inspired by or based on folksongs and folk dances or, at least, affected by some folk custom. As this style is closely linked to nineteenth-century nationalism and the folk movements belonging to that period (one of its most outstanding practitioners being Mussorgsky), it is proper to distinguish its twentieth-century appearance by naming it, as Stuckenshmidt suggested, 'neofolkism' or 'neofolklorism'. The movement has given creative inspiration and a coherent style to several composers during this century and as such takes its place among the major stylistic developments of modern music.

The compositional application of folk music was discussed and illustrated in Chapter Five. Three further points should be borne in mind. First, folk music provided several composers (among them Janáček, Bartók, Kodály and Vaughan Williams) with a national identity in sound and gave invigorating stimulus to their works. Secondly, as folk music is largely either modal or pentatonic, a renewed interest in these archaic and exotic scale structures was reflected in the thinking of some composers (for example Debussy, Bartók and Vaughan Williams). Thirdly, ostinato technique and, above all, the mixed metric and asymmetric rhythmic patterns so characteristic of the folk music of central Europe and the East revitalized composers' rhythmic writing and introduced patterns relatively alien to Western music (see the works of Stravinsky and Bartók).

The above points were stressed by Bartók in his *Autobiography* of 1921:

In 1907 at the instigation of Kodály I became acquainted with Debussy's work, studied it thoroughly and was greatly surprised to find in his music pentatonic phrases similar in character to those contained in our peasant music. I was sure these could be attributed to influences of folk music from Eastern Europe, very likely from Russia. Similar influences can be traced in Igor Stravinsky's work. It seems, therefore, that, in our age, modern music has developed along similar lines in countries geographically far away from each other. It has become rejuvenated under the influence of a kind of peasant music that has remained untouched by the musical creations of the last century.

In an article written in 1931 concerning the influence of peasant music on modern music Bartók distinguished three methods of using folk melodies: (a) the quotation of original folk melodies which are accompanied and/or elaborated further in the contexts of a more elaborate structure; (b) the composition of entirely new folk-like melodies based on a close imitation of the originals; (c) the writing of entirely original compositions which are nevertheless in the spirit of and thus evoke folk music.

Vaughan Williams, a collector of folksongs who had an eclectic outlook in music, questioned whether it is necessary to be original in music: 'The duty of the composer is to find the *mot juste*. It does not matter if this word has been said a thousand times before as long as it is the right thing to say at that moment.' Folk music is part of the musical vocabulary of a nation from which composers can select, if they wish, *le mot juste*. Originality, therefore, is not so much a matter of invention as one of choice and application.

Folk music, both indigenous and imported, has exercised and continues to exercise a profound influence on a variety of composers, from Stravinsky to Philip Glass. Even Britten, who was not a member of the Vaughan Williams school, composed the orchestral Suite on English Folk Tunes 'A Time There Was' Op. 90, which he dedicated to Percy Grainger, a folksong collector and composer.

It was written two years before Britten's death, and there is a swansong-like quality in his use of the folk idiom.

Bartók recognized the danger of chauvinistic nationalism which can so easily lurk behind folk studies. For this reason he extended his research to countries other than Hungary, thus fostering the cause of comparative studies in ethno-musicology. As we saw in Chapter Five, since 1945 musicians have increasingly absorbed the musical styles of other countries, especially those of non-European countries. Such composers as Berio, Cage, Messiaen, the American minimalists and Stockhausen, while they are not folklorists in the Bartókian sense, nevertheless show the fruitful absorption of folk elements taken from virtually all over the world.

Social realism

Ideologies, whether religious or socio-political, have always played a major role in the arts. For some this has been inspiring, for others limiting, if not crippling. Since ancient times rulers have been aware of the propaganda potential of the arts as well as of their subversive strength, so the arts have been both valued and looked at with suspicion by the tyrants of history. Furthermore, the idea that the arts can be deemed 'healthy' or 'unhealthy' according to some moral and psychological criteria goes back to at least the ancient Greeks. In music, for example, Plato gave preference to certain modes, which he believed were invigorating, positive and manly, whereas other modes were judged to be effeminate, decadent and lacking in moral fibre. The inevitable conclusion is that in order to maintain a healthy society these enfeebling tendencies in music must be curtailed, censored, suppressed or even eliminated. In our century, infested by fanatical ideologies largely inherited from the nineteenth century, artists found themselves, depending on their geographical placing and political conditions, swinging between freedom, or sometimes anarchy, and the most brutal oppression.

The Nazis were quick to recognize that art, when not forced into subservience to the state or party and its propaganda machinery, can be a threat to tyranny and a mouthpiece for opposition. The works of more or less all the eminent composers of the time were condemned as *Kulturbolschewismus* (cultural bolshevism); the list includes the names of Bartók, Hindemith, Schoenberg and Stravinsky. To this folly was added the racist censoring of the music of such Jewish composers as Mendelssohn.

In Russia the situation was, to start with, different. In the 1920s the Bolsheviks were in favour of modern art as they equated it with the revolutionary social developments taking place during that time. For a while it seemed that Russia was in the forefront of both social and artistic revolution. This state of invigorating artistic liberalism did not last long, however, as by the 1930s a most oppressive curtailment of artistic freedom had been introduced by Stalin. The Soviets rejected almost every aspect of modernism as 'formalist' (with the result that almost all artists worthy of the name were in one way or another persecuted), and to be guilty of formalism was to be guilty of writing music of an atonal, dissonant nature without a clearly recognizable melody. Musicians, who were publicly criticized, were forced to renounce these tendencies in favour of easy comprehensibility, optimism and propagandist utterances designed to promote communism. In order to achieve these aims a return to the nineteenth-century nationalist idiom was prescribed, based on tonality and the diatonic system. In a way the term 'neo-romanticism' could, with some justification, be applied. After the doctrine of social realism was put forward by Maxim Gorky in 1934, this term stuck as a label for the artistic style of the Soviet Union. That Shostakovich and Prokofiev managed to survive and create masterpieces under such restrictions not only proves Schoenberg's dictum that 'there is still much good music to be written in C major', but is also a vindication of the human spirit.

Collage

This is another term which has its origin in fine art. A painter working in this style assembles a picture based on a selection of various materials (newspapers, cloth, chunks of wood and so on) and then sticks it on to a canvas or other surface, such as hardboard. The first of these collages was created by Picasso in 1912. Collage in music means the superimposition of several quotations from other composers' works or miscellaneous musical sources, for instance dances, marches or songs, as may be found in Ives's orchestral works. In this, as in many other things, he was a pioneer. With the dawn of *musique concrète* and electronic music after the Second World War musical collage came into its own. Varèsc's *Poème électronique*, Berio's *Sinfonia*, Gerhard's Symphony No. 3, a 'collage' for tape and orchestra, and Davies's *Eight Songs for a Mad King* are representative examples.

Music theatre

It is fitting that the discussion of this hybrid genre follows collage as it is a primarily theatrical genre in which several elements of the arts may be amalgamated. A new kind of staged entertainment, it is characterized by the blending of music, drama, speech, dance and lighting effects. The overall style is usually expressionist in manner.

Earlier works in this genre are Schoenberg's *Pierrot lunaire*, for which the performer was originally dressed in the costume of a clown, Stravinsky's *Soldier's Tale*, in which the fable about a soldier's home-coming from the First World War is narrated and acted out with music, and Falla's *El retablo de maese Pedro*, based on Cervantes's *Don Quixote*, which uses puppets. Ravel's enchanting *L'Enfant et les sortilèges*, on the libretto of Colette, offers dancing, singing, a chorus and a sumptuous fairy-tale staging, and could also be categorized as music theatre.

It was during the 1950s and 1960s that this theatrical mongrel came particularly into vogue; it began in America, but quickly spread to Europe. In America Cage was among the first to experiment with music theatre and chance music in *Theatre Piece*. The minimalists also experimented, covering a whole range of expressions. The absurd may be found in Young's *Piano Piece for David Tudor No. 1*, where the pianist is asked to feed the piano with a 'bale of hay and a bucket of water'. In Glass's spectacular quasi-operatic compositions, such as *Einstein on the Beach*, collage techniques based on historical figures, including Queen Victoria, Freud and Stalin, are brought together with singing, dancing, acting and the recitation of nonsensical texts.

In Britain music theatre is associated largely with the names of Peter Maxwell Davies and Harrison Birtwistle. Davies's *Eight Songs for a Mad King*, a dramatization of George III's insanity, and *Vesalii icones*, in which Jesus' Calvary and anatomical drawings of Vesalius are brought to life by a dancer, are outstanding examples of this indefinable art form.

Kagel's surrealist music theatre pieces belong to this genre, as does Stockhausen's *Inori* for orchestra and mime, in which thirteen different ways of praying, selected from various cultures, are enacted.

Music theatre offers modern composers a most flexible and imaginative alternative to opera and incidental music in plays. This is a form in which modern eclecticism reigns supreme and in which everything, except dullness, is permitted.

Minimalism

This term came into currency during the 1960s, at first in connection with the painting and sculpture of the time. The American minimalists of the 1960s, such as Dan Flavin, Don Geode and

Frank Stella, could trace a distinguished ancestry back to Europe before the First World War as many of their views were anticipated by the Russian suprematists, headed by Kasimir Malevich and the constructivist Vladimir Tatlin, as well as by the dadaists. Their aim in art was clarity and understatement expressed in rectangular and cubic forms; they hoped to achieve immediacy by avoiding complexities and 'deep meanings'.

In the sphere of music the minimalists set out to reject the intricacies of the serial thinking which dominated the period after the Second World War. They propagated instead a return to tonality and modality in their most elementary forms; harmonic movements are reduced to the minimum while obstinate repetitions of rhythmic patterns and small diatonic melodic units are used. The music thus created is trimmed to its most elemental, the effect of which is not unlike some trance-inducing Oriental music, or some types of pop and rock music. But whereas minimalism in art influenced pop art, it was pop music which had some influence on minimalism in music. Herein lies its ready appeal to audiences. Early minimalist music of the 1960s and 1970s underwent, not surprisingly, a development which was similar to that of jazz. Both forms of music entered through back doors: jazz was practised in bars, nightclubs and bordellos, and minimalism established itself in private performances in attics and by being part of visual art exhibitions in galleries and the theatre. All the minimalist composers shared a profound dissatisfaction with what they saw as the stuffy ethos of conservatories and universities. They gravitated towards other art forms, such as painting, drama and dancing, and embraced jazz, pop music and the music of both Africa and the Orient. In these styles of music they found a freedom and an immediacy lacking in the ivory tower of serialist scholasticism which largely dominated the 1960s and 1970s. The composers who practise minimalism are La Monte Young, Terry Riley, Philip Glass, Steve Reich and John Adams. At this point it would be worth stressing that minimalism does not imply that the length of a composition is kept to a minimum as well. On the contrary, a piece can be as long as a Mahler symphony. What characterizes minimalism is the way in which short melodic and rhythmic patterns are obstinately repeated and organized with controlled improvisation within the diatonic system. A number of interesting technical devices were introduced by some of the minimalists, notably Reich's 'phasing' and Adams's 'gating'.

Phasing is based on the idea of using two tape recorders, one of which is put out of phase with the other at a chosen point in the piece, producing an imitative polyphonic texture like a canon. The best introductions to this style of writing are Reich's *It's Gonna Rain*, *Come Out*, *Piano Phase*, *Phase Patterns*, *Drumming* and *Clapping Music*.

Adams's technique works as follows: a repetitive piece of music in minimalist ostinato style goes through several keys by means not of modulations, but of what the composer calls gates. The sustaining pedal is held throughout each section up to the gating (that is, where the new key starts) and so on till the end. This method is used in Adams's *China Gates* and *Phrygian Gates*, both for solo piano.

Adams, one of the youngest of the American minimalists, is perhaps the most romantically inclined. His works display a full-hearted lyricism which he expresses in large-scale musical canvases, such as his *Harmonium* for orchestra and chorus. This is a setting of the poems 'Negative Love' by John Donne and 'Because I could not stop for Death' and 'Wild nights – wild nights!' by Emily Dickinson, and it is one of the most memorable compositions of the 1980s. Competing in interest are *Harmonielehre* (1985), which has a sense of spaciousness not unlike a vast musical landscape, and his opera *Nixon in China* (1987), which established him as one of the leading composers of his generation. With this work he spectacularly succeeded in writing an opera based on a contemporary political event. The grandiose banality and empty rhetoric of 'high-level' international meetings is superbly captured at the scene of Nixon's arrival at the airport, where he sings 'News has a kind of mystery'. The simple statement is rendered minimalist by the characteristic repetitive style: 'News news news news news news news news news news news news has a has a has a has a kind of mystery has a has a has a kind of mystery . . .'

To start with the minimalists were not well received by critics, who thought that the ostinato style was limited. They were proven wrong. After serialism had led expressionism to a dead end, something which had become apparent by the end of the 1970s, the minimalists offered a refreshingly imaginative return to tonality and an immediacy founded on a synthetic approach to music in which light and serious music and Western and Oriental elements are blended, giving the style an international flavour and comprehensibility.

Minimalism too will, in due course, be superseded by some other stylistic and technical development. And so it should be. In art there is no lasting monopoly for schools or styles. 'The unexpected is always upon us.'

Epilogue

When you reach this point of the book, I hope you will have had your appetite for further exploration of the realm of modern music whetted and that, equipped with some facts and a better understanding, you can do so with greater confidence. The Bibliography lists outstanding works concerning many aspects of twentieth-century music. As stressed at the beginning of this book, however, what matters when trying to appreciate music is to listen to it regularly with attention and empathy. The recognition of greatness and the value of art takes some practice. As the Preface was verbal, let me close the Epilogue with some music from Messiaen's *Quatuor pour la fin du temps*, which he composed in a prison camp, Stalag VIIIA, Görlitz Silesia, during the Second World War. In it he expresses his unfailing belief in spiritual values which for him were found in Christianity, made all the more significant because of the circumstances in which he wrote. The final movement, for violin and piano, is headed 'Louange à l'immortalité de Jésus'.

Fig. 199 >

Select Bibliography

Dictionaries

Apel, Willi, *Harvard Dictionary of Music*, Heinemann, 1970.

Griffiths, Paul, *The Thames and Hudson Encyclopedia of 20th-century Music*, Thames and Hudson, 1986.

Kennedy, Michael, *The Concise Oxford Dictionary of Music*, Oxford University Press, 1980.

McLeish, Kenneth, *The Penguin Companion to the Arts in the Twentieth Century*, Penguin, 1985.

Sadie, Stanley (ed.), *The New Grove Dictionary of Music and Musicians*, Macmillan, 1980.

History

Austin, William, *Music in the 20th Century (from Debussy through Stravinsky)*, Dent, 1966.

Déri, Ottó, *Exploring Twentieth-century Music*, Holt, Rinehart and Winston, 1968.

Griffiths, Paul, *Modern Music: The Avant Garde Since 1945*, Dent, 1981.

Griffiths, Paul, *Modern Music: A Concise History from Debussy to Boulez*, Thames and Hudson, 1987.

Grout, Donald, *A History of Western Music*, Dent, 1981.

Károlyi, Ottó, *Modern British Music: From Elgar to P. Maxwell Davies*, Associated University Presses, 1994.

Machlis, Joseph, *Introduction to Contemporary Music*, Dent, 1963.

Mellers, Wilfrid, *Man and His Music*, Barrie and Rockliff, 1962.

Mellers, Wilfrid, *Music in a New Found Land*, Oxford University Press, 1987.

Morgan, Robert, *Twentieth Century Music: A History of Musical Styles in Modern Europe and America*, Norton, 1991.

Salzman, Eric, *Twentieth-century Music: An Introduction*, Prentice-Hall, 1967.

Simms, Bryan, *Music in the Twentieth Century: Style and Structure*, Schirmer, 1986.

Whittall, Arnold, *Music Since the First World War*, Dent, 1977.

Theory

Bent, Ian, and Drabkin, William, *The New Grove Handbook in Music Analysis*, Macmillan, 1987.

Boretz, Benjamin, and Cone, Edward (eds), *Perspectives on Contemporary Music Theory*, Norton, 1972.

Boulez, Pierre, *Orientation*, Faber, 1986.

Brindle, Reginald Smith, *The New Music: The Avant-garde Since 1945*, Oxford University Press, 1975.

Campbell, Murray, and Greated, Clive, *The Musician's Guide to Acoustics*, Dent, 1987.

Cogan, Robert, *New Images of Musical Sound*, Harvard University Press, 1984.

Cole, Hugo, *Sounds and Signs: Aspects of Musical Notation*, Oxford University Press, 1974.

Cook, Nicholas, *A Guide to Musical Analysis*, Dent, 1987.

Cope, David, *New Directions in Music*, W. M. C. Brown, 1971.

Dahlhaus, Carl, *Schoenberg and the New Music*, Cambridge University Press, 1987.

Dunsley, Jonathan, and Whittall, Arnold, *Music Analysis in Theory and Practice*, Faber, 1988.

Forte, Allan, *The Structure of Atonal Music*, Yale University Press, 1973.

Griffiths, Paul, *A Guide to Electronic Music*, Thames and Hudson, 1979.

Howat, Roy, *Debussy in Proportion: A Musical Analysis*, Cambridge University Press, 1983.

Judd, F. C., *Electronic Music*, Neville Spearman, 1972.

Karkoschka, Erhard, *Notation in New Music*, Universal Edition, 1972.

Károlyi, Ottó, *Introducing Music*, Penguin, 1965.

Leibowitz, René, *Schoenberg and His School: The Contemporary Stage of the Language of Music*, Da Capo, 1975.

Lendvai, Ernő, *Béla Bartók: An Analysis of His Music*, Kahn and Averill, 1971.

Manning, Peter, *Electronic and Computer Music*, Clarendon Press, 1985.

Nyman, Michael, *Experimental Music: Cage and Beyond*, Studio Vista, 1974.

Perle, George, *Serial Composition and Atonality*, Faber, 1962.

Rastall, Richard, *The Notation of Western Music*, Dent, 1983.

Read, Gardner, *Contemporary Instrumental Techniques*, Schirmer, 1976.

Read, Gardner, *Modern Rhythmic Notation*, Gollancz, 1980.

Réti, Rudolf, *Tonality, Atonality, Pantonality: A Study of Some Trends in Twentieth-century Music*, Macmillan, 1958.

Rognoni, Luigi, *The Second Vienna School: Expressionism and Dodecaphony*, Calder, 1977.

Rufer, Josef, *Composition with Twelve Notes Related Only to One Another*, Barrie and Rockliff, 1954.

Schaefer, John, *New Sounds: The Virgin Guide to New Music*, Virgin, 1990.

Schoenberg, Arnold, *Style and Idea*, Faber, 1975.

Schwartz, Elliott, *Electronic Music: A Listeners' Guide*, Praeger, 1972.

Stockhausen, Karlheinz, *Stockhausen on Music*, Marion Boyars, 1989.

Strauss, Joseph, *Introduction to Post-tonal Theory*, Prentice-Hall, 1990.

Trythall, Gilbert, *Principles and Practice of Electronic Music*, 1973.

Ethnic and popular

Blesh, Rudi, *Shining Trumpet: A History of Jazz*, Da Capo, 1976.

Bohlman, Philip V., *The Study of Folk Music in the Modern World*, Indiana University Press, 1988.

Feather, Leonard, *From Satchmo to Miles*, Quartet, 1974.

Lyttelton, Humphrey, *The Best of Jazz*, Penguin, 1980.

May, Elizabeth (ed.), *Music of Many Cultures*, University of California Press, 1980.

Mellers, Wilfrid, *Twilight of the Gods: The Beatles in Retrospect*, Faber, 1971.

Melly, George, *Revolt into Style: The Pop Arts in Britain*, Penguin, 1970.

Palmer, Tony, *All You Need Is Love: The Story of Popular Music*, Futura, 1977.

Tirro, Franc, *Jazz: A History*, Norton, 1977.

General

Adorno, Theodor W., *Philosophy of Modern Music*, Seabury Press, 1973.

Apollonio, Umbro, *Futurist Manifestos*, Thames and Hudson, 1973.

Butler, Christopher, *After the Wake: An Essay on the Contemporary Avant-garde*, Clarendon Press, 1980.

Cage, John, *Silence*, Wesleyan University Press, 1961.

Dufallo, Richard, *Trackings: Composers Speak with Richard Dufallo*, Oxford University Press, 1989.

Langer, Susanne K., *Feeling and Form: A Theory of Art*, Routledge and Kegan Paul, 1953.

Mellers, Wilfrid, *Caliban Reborn: Renewal in Twentieth-century Music*, Harper and Row, 1967.

Meyer, Leonard B., *Emotion and Meaning in Music*, University of Chicago Press, 1956.

Meyer, Leonard B., *Music, the Arts, and Ideas*, University of Chicago Press, 1967.

Mitchell, Donald, *The Language of Modern Music*, Faber, 1963.

Palmer, Christopher, *Impressionism in Music*, Hutchinson, 1973.

Rockwell, John, *All American Music: Composition in the Late Twentieth Century*, Kahn and Averill, 1985.

Anthologies of music

Agay, Dènes, *An Anthology of Piano Music*, Vol. IV: *The Twentieth Century Major Composers of Our Time*, Yorktown Music Press, 1971.

Bartók, Béla, *Mikrokosmos*, Vols I–VI, Boosey and Hawkes, 1940.

Brant, William, *The Comprehensive Study of Music: Anthology of Music from Debussy through Stockhausen*, Harper's College Press, 1976.

Godwin, Joscelyn, *Schirmer Scores: A Repertory of Western Music*, Schirmer, 1975.

Kamien, Roger, *The Norton Scores: An Anthology for Listening*, Vol. 2, Norton, 1977.

Simms, Bryan, *Music of the Twentieth Century: An Anthology*, Schirmer, 1986.

Universal Edition, *Styles in 20th Century Piano Music*, Universal Edition, 1968.

Index

Discover more about our forthcoming books through Penguin's FREE newspaper...

Penguin
Quarterly

It's packed with:

- exciting features
- author interviews
- previews & reviews
- books from your favourite films & TV series
- exclusive competitions & much, much more...

READ MORE IN PENGUIN

In every corner of the world, on every subject under the sun, Penguin represents quality and variety – the very best in publishing today.

For complete information about books available from Penguin – including Puffins, Penguin Classics and Arkana – and how to order them, write to us at the appropriate address below. Please note that for copyright reasons the selection of books varies from country to country.

In the United Kingdom: Please write to *Dept. JC, Penguin Books Ltd, FREEPOST, West Drayton, Middlesex UB7 OBR.*

If you have any difficulty in obtaining a title, please send your order with the correct money, plus ten per cent for postage and packaging, to *PO Box No. 11, West Drayton, Middlesex UB7 OBR*

In the United States: Please write to *Consumer Sales, Penguin USA, P.O. Box 999, Dept. 17109, Bergenfield, New Jersey 07621-0120.* VISA and MasterCard holders call 1-800-253-6476 to order all Penguin titles

In Canada: Please write to *Penguin Books Canada Ltd, 10 Alcorn Avenue, Suite 300, Toronto, Ontario M4V 3B2*

In Australia: Please write to *Penguin Books Australia Ltd, P.O. Box 257, Ringwood, Victoria 3134*

In New Zealand: Please write to *Penguin Books (NZ) Ltd, Private Bag 102902, North Shore Mail Centre, Auckland 10*

In India: Please write to *Penguin Books India Pvt Ltd, 706 Eros Apartments, 56 Nehru Place, New Delhi 110 019*

In the Netherlands: Please write to *Penguin Books Netherlands bv, Postbus 3507, NL-1001 AH Amsterdam*

In Germany: Please write to *Penguin Books Deutschland GmbH, Metzlerstrasse 26, 60594 Frankfurt am Main*

In Spain: Please write to *Penguin Books S. A., Bravo Murillo 19, 1° B, 28015 Madrid*

In Italy: Please write to *Penguin Italia s.r.l., Via Felice Casati 20, I–20124 Milano*

In France: Please write to *Penguin France S. A., 17 rue Lejeune, F–31000 Toulouse*

In Japan: Please write to *Penguin Books Japan, Ishikiribashi Building, 2–5–4, Suido, Bunkyo-ku, Tokyo 112*

In Greece: Please write to *Penguin Hellas Ltd, Dimocritou 3, GR–106 71 Athens*

In South Africa: Please write to *Longman Penguin Southern Africa (Pty) Ltd, Private Bag X08, Bertsham 2013*

READ MORE IN PENGUIN

A SELECTION OF MUSICAL HITS

American Heartbeat Mick Brown

Haunted since childhood by the titles, lyrics and places of classic hit songs such as 'Chattanooga Choo-Choo', 'Memphis Tennessee', 'Twenty-four Hours from Tulsa' and 'Do You Know the Way to San José?', Mick Brown set out on a musical journey to discover the reality behind the myth. With wit and insight, he captures the essence of each town and city to build up a portrait of America and its rapidly changing society.

Feel Like Going Home Peter Guralnick

Ranging from the blues giants Muddy Waters and Howlin' Wolf to the storming blues-based Memphis rock 'n' roll of Jerry Lee Lewis and Charlie Rich, *Feel Like Going Home* is the unmissable first part of Peter Guralnick's monumental tribute to the roots of American popular music.

Shots from the Hip Charles Shaar Murray

His classic encapsulation of the moment when rock stars turned junkies as the sixties died; his dissection of rock 'n' roll violence as citizens assaulted the Sex Pistols; his superstar encounters from the decline of Paul McCartney to Mick Jagger's request that the author should leave – Charles Shaar Murray's *Shots from the Hip* is also rock history in the making.

In the Fascist Bathroom Greil Marcus

'More than seventy short pieces on "punk", its fall-out and its falling-outs. They are mostly brilliant . . . much of this book is hate as love, spite as delight. But when the professor does fall in love . . . he is a joy to behold' – *Sunday Times*

Dylan: Behind the Shades Clinton Heylin

'The most accurately researched and competently written account of Dylan's life yet . . . Heylin allots equal space to each of the three decades of Dylan's career, and offers a particularly judicious assessment of his achievements in the post-conversion Eighties' – *London Review of Books*

READ MORE IN PENGUIN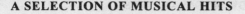

A SELECTION OF MUSICAL HITS

The Dark Stuff   Nick Kent
Selected Writings on Rock Music 1972–1993

Never afraid to flirt with danger and excess, Nick Kent didn't just know how to write about rock stars ... he lived in their shadow. From the debauched turbulence of the Rolling Stones on tour, to the violence that surrounded the Sex Pistols, from the tragedies of Brian Wilson and Syd Barrett to the epic survival sagas of Neil Young and Iggy Pop, Nick Kent got close to everything that was mad, bad and dangerous to know about rock 'n' roll.

Keith Richards   Victor Bockris

'Victor Bockris, who wrote brilliant biographies of Andy Warhol and Cassius Clay, is the biographer Richards deserves; a fluid, supple, generous writer who never descends into puffery or ascends into sarcasm ... Richards and Bockris are definitely as good as it gets' – *Spectator*

Pet Shop Boys versus America   Chris Heath

In 1991 the Pet Shop Boys – the pop group notorious for its humour, intelligence and prudence in the face of stardom – went to tour America, the land that idolizes the famous. The book that resulted (with pictures by Pennie Smith) is a gripping document of modern celebrity.

The American Night   Jim Morrison

'A hellfire preacher, part-terrified, part-enraged and mainly fascinated by the drawbacks that being merely human entails ... refreshing' – *Sunday Times*. 'A great American poet' – Oliver Stone

Unforgettable Fire: The Story of U2   Eamon Dunphy

When *The Joshua Tree* topped the charts in twenty-two countries, U2 became the hottest band in the world. 'Zoo TV' took their fame to sublime heights. Half Catholic, half Protestant, the band embodies the conflict and anguish of a divided Ireland – across the world their music is the voice of hope for millions. '*Unforgettable Fire* is a beacon ... in a cynical world' – *Time Out*

READ MORE IN PENGUIN

MUSIC REFERENCE

The Penguin Guide to Compact Discs and Cassettes
Ivan March, Edward Greenfield, Robert Layton

'Within the space of a few years *The Penguin Guide* has become something of an institution, its status earned largely through a cheerful, informative "plain speaking" style, copious entries, and attractive reader-friendly presentation' – *CD Review*

Introducing Music   Otto Karolyi

'Here is one of those rare things – an instruction book that seems to succeed completely in what it sets out to do ... The author develops the reader's knowledge of the language and sense of music to the stage where he can both follow ... a full score, and even make sense of some of the exceedingly complex programme notes' – *Recorder*

The Penguin Book of Rock & Roll Writing   Edited by Clinton Heylin

'A welcome and lovingly compiled reminder of different people in different times' – Nick Hornby. 'All our rock yesterdays in a stimulating anthology' – *Esquire*

The Penguin Dictionary of Music   Arthur Jacobs

A comprehensive and exceptionally wide-ranging work of reference, *The Penguin Dictionary of Music* covers opera and ballet as well as orchestral, solo, choral and chamber music. It is indispensable for anyone with an interest in music – whether professionally or purely for enjoyment.

The Penguin Guide to Jazz on CD, LP and Cassette
Richard Cook and Brian Morton

'An incisive account of available recordings which cuts across the artificial boundaries by which jazz has been divided ... each page has a revelation; everybody will find their own' – *The Times*